MEN WORTH KNOWING

Other books by J. Ellsworth Kalas
from Westminster John Knox Press

Grace in a Tree Stump: Old Testament Stories of God's Love
Preaching the Calendar: Celebrating Holidays and Holy Days

MEN WORTH KNOWING

BIBLICAL MEDITATIONS
FOR DAILY LIVING

J. Ellsworth Kalas

Westminster John Knox Press
LOUISVILLE • LONDON

Scripture quotations, unless otherwise indicated, are from the New Revised Standard Version of the Bible, copyright © 1989 by the Division of Christian Education of the National Council of the Churches of Christ in the U.S.A., and used by permission.

"Stubborn Ounces (To One Who Doubts the Worth of Doing Anything if You Can't Do Everything)" from *Hands Laid Upon the Wind,* by Bonaro W. Overstreet, Copyright © 1955 by W. W. Norton & Co. Inc. Used by permission of W. W. Norton & Company, Inc.

Book design by Sharon Adams
Cover design by Night & Day Design

First edition
Published by Westminster John Knox Press
Louisville, Kentucky

This book is printed on acid-free paper that meets the American National Standards Institute Z39.48 standard. ∞

PRINTED IN THE UNITED STATES OF AMERICA

07 08 09 10 11 12 13 14 15 16 — 10 9 8 7 6 5 4 3 2 1

Library of Congress Cataloging-in-Publication Data is on file at the Library of Congress, Washington, D.C.

ISBN-13: 978-0-664-23059-3
ISBN-10: 0-664-23059-8

Contents

Preface   vii

1. The Original Optimist (Genesis 3:8–20)   1
2. Just an Ordinary Man (Genesis 5:18–24)   8
3. The Boy Who Grew into His Coat (Genesis 37)   15
4. The Man Moses (Exodus 2:1–22)   22
5. A Man after God's Own Heart (1 Samuel 16:1–12)   29
6. My Friend, Elijah (1 Kings 19:1–12)   36
7. "Stubborn Ounces" (Amos 7:10–17)   43
8. Faithful for the Long Pull (Daniel 6:1–10)   50
9. Living on Borrowed Time (Luke 2:25–35)   58
10. Friend of the Bridegroom (John 1:6–9; 3:22–30)   65
11. The Soldier-Theologian (Matthew 8:5–13
    [Luke 7:1–10])   72
12. An Obscure Hero (John 8:1–11)   79
13. "Rock" for a Reason (Matthew 16:13–23)   86
14. Young Man in a Hurry (Acts 12:6–12)   95
15. A Rare Friend (2 Timothy 1:15–17)   102
16. "A Gardener among Human Beings"
    (Acts 11:19–26)   109

Notes   117

Preface

Very long ago, my youthful idealism was momentarily upset when an older friend advised me to seek out a certain person by saying, "He's someone worth knowing." When the friend saw my reaction, he quickly explained that he wasn't using the phrase in the sense of someone who would give me economic, political, or social advantage. Quite the opposite: this was the kind of person who would make me want to be a better human being.

I thank God for all such persons whose lives have intersected mine. I have known them at all levels of performance, from the simple and naive to the complex and profound, and at every measure of distance—including those individuals I have known only through history, hearsay, and the printed page.

Among those I have met through the printed page, none have influenced me as profoundly as the people I have met through the Bible. These persons got an early start on a boy who was taught to revere the Scriptures and for whom therefore these persons were much larger than life-size.

As time went by I realized that, to the contrary, these Bible personalities were made of the same stuff as the rest of us, and that their wonder was not in how different they were from the mass of humanity but in their sometimes grand and sometimes stumbling resemblance.

I am delighted to be able to bring some of these wonderful biblical men to your attention. I hope, first of all, that you will feel as you read that you do, indeed, *know* these men; and then that you like them, and that through this association you are learning from them—not only through their wisdom but sometimes through their errors and their obvious humanness.

And with it all, I hope they will add new quality to your walk with God.

J. Ellsworth Kalas

Chapter 1

The Original Optimist

Scripture Reading: Genesis 3:8–20

I want to say a good word for one of our ancestors. To be specific, our oldest ancestor, Adam—the one we credit with beginning it all. Adam generally gets a bad rap, and in a sense he earned it. As the Bible tells the story, Adam got all of us in a mess of trouble. The human race, Genesis reports, were to be lofty creatures, but then Adam and Eve began listening to an extraordinary traveling sales-man, and our race fell. So we've been blaming our troubles on Adam ever since. Theologians have a word for it: they speak of our "Adamic nature." By this they mean our tendency to get into trouble, our nasty side, the part of us that is especially susceptible to sin.

But I want to say a good word for Adam. I do this partly because it isn't wise to constantly bad-mouth our ancestors. They belong to us and we belong to them, whether we like it or not, so we do well to stand by them. Therefore I speak a good word for Adam. As I see it, he was not only our first named ancestor, he was the first optimist. And as someone who likes upbeat people, I am thus predisposed to look favorably on Adam.

Let me tell you more of his story, to give you a background for this father of optimism. The first time we hear of Adam, he is without a name. Near the end of the creation story, God said, "Let us make humankind in our image, according to our likeness," to exercise authority over the whole creation.

> So God created humankind in his image,
> in the image of God he created them;
> male and female he created them (Gen. 1:27).

God liked what he had done. In the earlier process of creation, according to the Genesis account, God said again and again, "This is good." But when God finished with the human creatures, the divine evaluation was, "This is *very* good." Well, in truth the human beings had better be "very good," because they were going to be God's first assistants in running the singular planet called Earth. God put them in charge. It was a planet in wonderfully perfect operating order, and when you have such a good system you don't want to trust it to just anyone; you want someone really competent, so you get someone like this first team.

Now if in your reading of the Bible you sometimes look at the footnotes, you may have seen that what is translated in Genesis 1:27 as "humankind" is in the Hebrew *adam*. And as the story unfolds, we begin calling the man by that name.

Before long, Adam and the woman with whom God blessed him went astray. One day a virtual stranger, but a very attractive, very persuasive one, approached them and suggested that they didn't really have a very good deal. We humans are a peculiar lot. It hardly matters how fortunate our personal state may be, we can be convinced very easily that we should be treated better. It sounds as if we had this inclination even before sin became part of our nature, but I won't get into that just now. At any rate, Adam let his wife take over the conversation. Under the circumstances, this was very unfortunate, because God had specifically warned Adam against a particular hazard, and the stranger was trying to sell the couple on violating God's counsel by taking some of the forbidden fruit. Knowing what he did, Adam should have spoken up. He should have said, "This conversation really needs to end right now, because its ultimate destination is trouble." Instead, Adam remained silent. He failed to assume his spiritual responsibility.

As a result, Adam and his wife did the thing—the *one thing!*—God had told them not to do. A curse then came upon them. The woman would have pain in childbearing. The man would find that the ground was cursed. It would still bring forth food, but it would also bring forth thorns and thistles, and humans would earn their living by the sweat of their brow. Previously it could be said of life, "No sweat"; now, sweat would be a way of life, a prerequisite to earning a living.

So the dream had gone smash. Where once there had been vegetables, grain, and flowers, now these favors were interspersed with weeds. You can imagine it happening even as God speaks. Adam's eyes are downcast, but within their range his eyes have seen roses and wheat and cucumbers; now, even as he looks, thistles spring up in the midst of the wheat; and over there, where a vine is bearing lush grapes, kudzu begins to swallow it up.

In truth, however, this is not the worst of Adam's troubles. The weeds in his garden are nothing compared to the weeds in his soul. He used to look forward to God's evening visits in the garden; now Adam dreads the thought that God might appear, because he knows that the friendship isn't what it used to be. Previously, he was in perfect communion with his wife; she was bone of his bone and flesh of his flesh. Now, however, he looks on her somewhat skeptically, because he has an idea that she is the source of all his troubles. In this, of course, he is the ancestor of several men I've met, who look at their wives the same way. Adam used to be a supremely happy guy, in love with his garden, in love with his wife, in love with his God, and in love with his life. He used to awaken every day wanting to sing, "Oh, what a beautiful morning!" Now he's not sure, because he doesn't know what the day will bring forth. Everything is somehow out of joint. He can't believe what has happened to his beautiful, perfect world.

Then Adam looks at the woman, his wife, and it dawns on him that she doesn't have a name. I don't know why he was so long delayed in coming to this realization, since God had entrusted him with naming the animals. So he may be late in coming to the realization, but now he senses he can't go on just saying, "Woman!" or worse, "Hey, you!" She must have a name. And just as quickly, Adam knows what it should be. He will call her "Eve." Why? Because in the Hebrew "Eve" sounds like "living," and Adam says that this woman is "the mother of all living" (Gen. 3:20).

That's why I call Adam an optimist. He has only recently received a death sentence. Having been created as someone who might live forever, he and his wife are now under a death sentence. Still more complicating, they have been evicted from their home, and have been told that the years of life still lying before them are going to be made difficult by weeds, pain in childbirth, and sweaty work. Worst of all, the one who got them into trouble, that stranger, their adversary, is still around. Who knows what further trouble he will bring them? After all, if he could persuade them to rebel against the God who had provided for them so generously, he could sell them almost anything. Besides, now that life is more complicated, they might be more susceptible than ever to the sales pitch of this troublemaker. Everything has gone wrong for this couple: they've lost their home and they are under a death sentence. So now Adam says, "I know what I'll call this woman! I will call her *"Life-giver! Eve!"* And he did.

Now there's an optimist for you. Don Marquis, the poet and journalist, said that "an optimist is a guy that has never had much experience." In a way, Adam fits that definition, because his experience was limited; but you have to admit that the experience he had was of a monumental kind, so he wasn't likely just now to see life as all sunshine. To be painfully honest, after the trouble Adam and his wife had just gotten into, and with her seeming to have led the way, he might easily have decided to call his wife "Trouble." Or maybe, living as they did toward the south and with a southern inclination for two given names, he might have called her "Bad News." But instead, Adam called her "Life-giver." I think that's wonderful.

But just where did Adam get such optimism? How could he be so hopeful in the wake of so many lost dreams? The obvious explanation, of course, is that he sensed that his wife was going to be the bearer of life to the next generation. He must have understood that God had so equipped her that in her womb she would receive and shelter life. He might have the gift of life in his semen, but it would be an unfinished gift unless it could be joined with another and deposited in a uniquely nurturing place, and God had given that unique place and ministry to the woman. Call her, therefore, "Life-giver."

That's a logical explanation, and I accept it as far as it goes. But, in truth, I'm looking for something more. As you well know, we humans don't manage our lives entirely on the systems and syllogisms of logic. And here's what I see in Adam's story as I look more deeply. When things were so confused and hopeless for that bewildered couple, Adam might easily have concluded that life wasn't worth bothering with. He could have been content simply to let the lights go out with his story: why bother to carry on something when the promise has gone out of it, when the best has been lost? Why bother with life, if life holds so little hope? If you've lost paradise, why make shift with what's left? You can revise the song Peggy Lee made famous a generation ago and say, "Since that's all there is, I don't care to have it."

But, instead, Adam looked at his wife, smiled, then shouted, "I have a name for you, woman! You are *Life-giver!*"

Why did he say it? There has to be some logic in this man's response, something more than just pulling himself up by his sandal straps. What made him speak as he did?

Quite simply, because he had once lived in Eden. Adam began, not on some back street, not in some rundown neighborhood, not even in a fairly good starter home. Adam began in *paradise*, in Eden. And he couldn't forget it.

Friend, we should never forget where we started. Now understand me: I realize that we are a fallen race, and there's no doubt about it. If you ever wonder if we're fallen, just listen to the evening news, or read the news in the paper and on the Web. We're a bit of a mess. We're a fallen race.

But that isn't where we started. You and I *started* in Eden. That was our original human address. Mind you, I'm not talking biology at this moment, or the recorded history of the human race. I'm talking what every human being senses deep within; I'm talking the loveliest of theology, and the best of faith, and the most beautiful of poetry. I'm saying that we humans are the best part of God's dream, which means that our original human address was Eden. And by the grace of God, we still have some vestigial remains of that paradise at work in our souls. That's what makes us optimists.

Let me give you some for-instances of what I mean. Let's start with politics, since we get a pretty steady diet of that subject year in and year out. After centuries of history—centuries of war, dictators, and often-dishonest leaders—we keep on believing in politics. Why do we keep thinking that the Berlin walls should fall, that subjugated peoples should get a vote (even when a pathetically large portion of our own voting population fails to use its privilege)? After (in the language of politics) we've thrown the rascals out, why do we think the team we bring in will be better? Hasn't history made us cynics? Why do we keep listening to political speeches in America, and why do people rally around a new hope in settings where to do so may cost them their lives?

I'll tell you why. Because there's something of Eden in us, something that says that next year, next election, next king, next mayor, things will be better. In that wonderful play and movie, *Camelot*, the best dreams of King Arthur go smash. His finest soldier and his wife, Guinevere, betray him with an adulterous relationship. Camelot, the dream empire, is on the verge of collapsing, besieged by enemy armies and already disastrously corrupted within. But as the story ends a boy comes to King Arthur, volunteering his services to the king because he wants to keep Camelot alive. It is a beautifully symbolic ending for the movie: at a point when the dream has crashed, a new generation appears in the form of a slip of a boy, to keep the dream alive. I suspect that every political campaign includes some politicians who are greedy and self-seeking, but I'm just as sure that there is always a new generation of idealists—people who believe that they or their candidate will make a difference. Every time I see such idealism in a young person—or an old one, for that matter—I say to myself, "We're still looking for Eden! We still have this irrational idea that we can make a paradise." The blood of Eden flows in our veins.

Or think of love and romance. Marriage has surely taken a beating in this past generation. Divorce seems to be the rule of the day. Some sociologists suggest that we should plan on starter marriages just as we plan on a starter home, figuring we will do better the second or third time. Several years ago I saw a clever saying in a little bookstore; I don't know the author's name, so I can't give credit. Listen: "What I know about love is what a three-legged dog knows about automobiles." A great many people might tell you that those words summarize their story.

Nevertheless, people go on falling in love and getting married. Some degree of pessimism has set in, but I marvel that we humans keep thinking like Adam, that some person is their missing rib, bone of their bone and flesh of their flesh! Every year tens of thousands of young people who have grown up in homes where there was more fighting than love somehow are optimistic enough to think they will have a better home. They fall in love, and with sublime, perhaps irrational, optimism think it will work for them when in truth they've never seen it work for anyone.

So where did Adam get the optimism to name the woman "Eve"? It's because he was born in Eden, and he never fully got over it. And neither have you and I. Fallen as we are, beaten as have been by sin and human folly, we are still descendants of a divine plan that began with perfection. Optimism comes naturally to us, because our roots are in Eden. We don't live there anymore, but we know the street, we remember the place where we started. We've lost our way, but we still have an instinct for the old home place.

You are I are the sons and daughters of the original optimist, who, having received the death penalty, named the woman he loved "Lifegiver." And because this optimistic ancestor of ours was born in Eden, you and I somehow continue to know that Eden is our original address. It's the old home place.

Chapter 2

Just an Ordinary Man

Scripture Lesson: Genesis 5:18–24

*I*n the nearly forty years that I was a pastor, I had scores of funeral or memorial services for persons who were good but unremarkable. When I would meet prior to the service with their children or a surviving spouse, they would describe the person in ordinary terms. Perhaps it was because these bereaved had no poetic gifts of expression, but I suspect it was more often because they didn't have too much material to work on. "He was a good father," a son or daughter would say. "Always there when I needed him." "A good man," a friend says. "Nothing spectacular, mind you, but good."

But as the years have gone by and I have observed the stuff that ultimately shapes life and history, I've decided there's nothing ordinary about goodness, and that nothing is so remarkable as a good life. It's usually only after such ordinary folks are gone that we begin to realize how special they were and how much we miss their simple goodness.

It's with that fact in mind that I want to examine one of the strangest stories in the Bible. Well, in truth it's hardly a story. It's really nothing more than a very brief biography in the midst of a series of death notices. You'll find it in the fifth chapter of the book of Genesis. I sometimes refer to it as the Obituary Page, because it is nothing other than a rather dismal listing of the births and deaths of some ancient personalities. The accounts are completely stylized. If you've read the fifth chapter of Genesis, you know what I mean. In each instance we read that a given person was born, then lived so many years until having a first child, after which they lived so many more years, having other children; and then, always, the same, inevitable conclusion: *"and he died."* In truth, it can be a rather desolate reading experience, and you're glad the chapter is no longer than it is.

But along the way this dreary recitation takes a dramatic, unannounced turn, with a man named Enoch. It starts like all the others: "When Enoch had lived sixty-five years, he became the father of Methuselah." It's then that the story line, different from all the others, turns. Listen: "Enoch walked with God after the birth of Methuselah three hundred years, and had other sons and daughters. Thus all the days of Enoch were three hundred sixty-five years. Enoch walked with God; then he was no more, because God took him" (Gen. 5:22–24).

At this point, of course, you want to argue with me about my description of Enoch. There's nothing ordinary about a person who makes such an extraordinary exit from our planet. As the writer of Genesis reports it, it sounds as if Enoch never really died; he just got special transportation to the next world. That makes him seem not only extraordinary, but, in the truest sense of the word, unique. Scholars of several kinds—theologians and students of literature, among others—have offered various opinions about what the Bible actually means when it says, "Then he was no more, because God took him." I certainly won't claim to have a final answer for you, but of this we can both be sure: the end to Enoch's earthly journey was altogether out of the ordinary.

But other than that, from all I can see, Enoch's life was average. Not in God's sight, obviously, or Enoch wouldn't have come to such a dramatic conclusion. But I have a feeling that if you and I had lived in Enoch's area, we probably wouldn't have noticed anything about him that would have attracted our special attention. I think the Bible makes that clear by what it doesn't say. That is, the Bible doesn't give us any record of his achievements. We don't know that he was a leader. There's no indication that he was a success by any particular measure, and it's not as if the Bible hesitates to tell us about people's achievements. For instance, it reports that Job was the greatest person in all of the east, and it makes clear that David was a great warrior, and Samuel a sterling leader, and Ezra a faithful scholar. But there's no such report on Enoch. All that we read here is that he "walked with God." I don't want to make a poor pun, but that's a pretty pedestrian report. Some years ago an Episcopal priest, Malcolm Boyd, became well known for a book he titled, *Are You Running with Me, Jesus?* Enoch wouldn't have qualified for such a title. He wasn't a runner. He just *walked* with God. I really doubt that we would have noticed him if we had been one of his neighbors; there's no evidence he would have attracted our attention or admiration.

But, somewhere along the way, something must have happened to Enoch that made him different—different, that is, in the eyes of God. How is it that this man—who, as far as we're told, saved no souls, preached no sermons, wrote no books, built no churches or synagogues, and to whom no particular good works are attributed—got to exit this life like no one else? The writer of Genesis gives us only the barest story. He tells us just one thing about Enoch that made him different from the others: that he "walked with God."

The New Testament adds a brief commentary to Enoch's story. The writer of the Letter to the Hebrews says that Enoch "pleased God," and that he did so because he had faith. Then the New Testament writer does us a big favor. He tells us something specific about faith, something that he is reminded of, apparently, by Enoch's experience. He says, "And without faith it is impossible to please God, for whoever would approach him must believe that he exists and that he rewards those who seek him" (Heb. 11:6). Enoch not only believed that God existed—that's pretty minimal, after all, and it doesn't require a great stretch of logic or imagination, but it's a starting point. More than that, Enoch believed that God rewards those who seek him. That is, Enoch had confidence in the character and the justice and the wondrous goodness of God.

So Enoch walked with God because he enjoyed God's company. If I may put it this way, Enoch felt that God was the kind of person he enjoyed being around. He was sure that God's intentions for him were good. Come to think of it, that's what we all look for in friends: we want to know that they're always in our corner, ready to rejoice when we're rejoicing and to weep when we weep.

All of us think that it's a good idea to walk with God. We feel it would be wonderful to have a substantial devotional life. We admire those persons who live so close to God that we call them saints. So why don't all of us walk with God? Quite simply, because we don't believe in God that much. We aren't as convinced of God's reality, or of God's goodness. We can't really imagine that God wants so much to have our company that we would be doing a beautiful thing if we put forth special effort to spend more time in the divine presence.

I remember a morning many years ago when I understood, deep within, that God wanted my company. It was my habit every morning to meet with God in front of my fireplace, just after I had brushed my teeth, washed my face, and shaved. One morning while I was shaving a voice inside me (I should confess that I've never heard an audible message from God, but this message was as good as audible), a voice spoke to my soul: "I'm waiting downstairs for you, you know." I hope you will take this for what it is worth, the report of a fellow pilgrim: for the first time in my life it occurred to me that God enjoyed my company, and that he cherished our morning conversations. It also dawned on me that in these morning meetings, I never had to wait for God; God was always there first.

But how is it that Enoch came to incline toward God as he did? Some would answer, "Because God planned it that way." Sorry, that's just too easy. Such reasoning prevents our getting beyond superficial thinking, and worse, it excuses us from taking responsibility for our own spiritual development. Besides, I don't see how God could have found any satisfaction in Enoch's faith if he had such faith simply because God made him that way. That would be like getting affection from an automaton.

I find a significant hint in the way the writer of Genesis tells the story. He says that Enoch became the father of Methuselah, and that he "walked with God after the birth of Methuselah three hundred years." Did the birth of his firstborn make a difference to Enoch? Did the wonder of it strike some previously untouched chord in his soul? All of the others in this obituary chapter—Seth, Kenan, Mahalalel, Jared—had children, and nothing like this happened to them. How is it that when Enoch had a son, he began then to walk with God?

I can't prove it, but I'm fully convinced that each of us has moments in life where there's the possibility of our turning a sacred corner. Moses saw a burning bush. Some scholars say that there's a bush in that part of the world that often gives such an appearance. I know nothing of that, and surely wouldn't seek to explain Moses' experience that way. But from my experience with human nature I submit that other persons through the years must have seen something that *could* have made them pause and listen for the voice of God. I wonder, even (forgive me some pure speculation), if Moses might himself have seen a burning bush earlier if he had been ready to see it? Alfred Tennyson saw a flower "in the crannied wall," and suddenly realized that if he could understand that flower—"What you are, root and all, and all in all"—he would know what God is, and what we human beings are. We think the flower is a thing to be plucked, or fertilized; Tennyson saw more. Elizabeth Barrett Browning realized that "Earth's crammed with heaven, / And every common bush afire with God." And perhaps there's the rub: most of the time we see that the bush is common without seeing that it is "afire with God."

I'm insisting that each of us has those moments in life that beg for spiritual experience. For some, it's the birth of a child. For others, it's losing a job or the end of a marriage. For still others, it's a choir anthem on a Sunday morning, or a sentence in a sermon that seems suddenly to stand alone. These corners that you and I turn, that all of us turn at one time or another, are times that are rich in the possibilities of meeting God. Enoch did, and that made all the difference.

As far as the biblical story is concerned, Enoch continued after that to live a very ordinary life. The Bible says simply that he "had other sons and daughters," just like the other persons in the obituary chapter. Walking with God didn't mean that he moved out of the everyday world of work, friendships, marriage, sex, and parenting.

Yet somehow Enoch found time and energy for walking with God. I wonder if it ever became a point of discussion with his neighbors. Did some of them say, "When I woke up early yesterday, I noticed a lamp burning in your house. What were you doing up so early?" "Praying." And did they look at him as someone strange, or did some of them say, "I don't know how you find the time. I don't have time for things like that."

I don't think those other people—Enoch's neighbors, or his ancestors or descendants—were necessarily bad people. They were just people who missed the point of life. There's no reason to think they were demonstrably wicked, those people who had children, then died. In any event, they're more to be pitied than censured, because they didn't get from life what life is most about. That's tragic, isn't it, that we should live our lives on this earth like ants hurrying madly in and out of our ant holes (except that our ant holes are equipped with television and computers, and they're air-conditioned) and that we miss the chance to walk with God!

The Bible says that Enoch walked with God, and then he was no more, because God "took him." In a sense, that's not surprising. If a person gets close enough to God, often enough, of course God "takes" him or her. We are captured by God. What Enoch knew physically, untold millions have come to know in allegory. Walk close to God, and God will, indeed, take you! "The things of earth will grow strangely dim / In the light of his glory and grace."[1]

Let me put it another way. When Enoch walked with God, he was exposed to life, to that special quality of life that is to be found only in the source of life, in God. This word, life, has so many definitions, you know—so many measures of depth and height and breadth. Now and again people come to the end of their days on earth expressing regret that they never really "lived"; on the other hand, people sometimes refer to some rare moment when it seems they have gotten so much life that they wouldn't be able to contain themselves if they were to experience such life on a daily or an hourly basis. Well, when we read that Enoch walked with God, we must understand that he was experiencing a quality of life that was quite other than what his neighbors knew. Knowing such life from day to day, is it so surprising that he simply exited from this life into eternal life? For all the others in the obituary chapter of Genesis, and for all of Enoch's contemporaries, death was a quite predictable conclusion to the way they were walking. This was the destination toward which their common steps were taken. Consider it: if we walk with death and lostness and confusion and sin, we can expect that death will be our destination. But if we walk with life, we will, of course, at the end walk right off into life. John Wesley said of the early Methodists, "Our people die well." Of course! They lived abundantly, so they died abundantly. Since Jesus said, "I came that they may have life, and have it abundantly," I would be disappointed if that abundance didn't extend to the end of life too.

I don't know if they had funeral or memorial services in Enoch's day. Cultural historians say that some sort of departure celebration for the dead is about as old as our human race, so I'm certain there was some sort of event, though it's hard to calculate what exactly it would be in an instance like Enoch's. As someone who has conducted hundreds of services, I try to imagine what I would have said at a service for Enoch. I think I would have described him as the patron saint of the routine. Everything about his life, it appears, was like that of all the other persons listed in the fifth chapter of Genesis. He too had a first child, and then a succession of others.

But after the birth of that first child, Enoch *walked with God.* And that, believe me, is the greatest achievement of which a human being is capable.

Don't think me a naive sentimentalist when I suggest that Enoch's spiritual descendants are with us still. I'm altogether certain that I've conducted services for any number of them. Obviously, they haven't been privileged to exit this earth in the way Enoch did, but that doesn't diminish their holy stature. Because, you see, the final measure of Enoch isn't really the way he left, but the way he lived. All that we know about him is quite ordinary, except for the wonderfully simple, wonderfully mysterious statement that he walked with God. There's nothing spectacular about that.

Or is there?

Chapter 3

The Boy Who Grew into His Coat

Scripture Lesson: Genesis 37

I'm sure every older generation is convinced that the new generation is spoiling its children. For those who decry child rearing on such generational terms, I direct you back a hundred generations or more to one of the great child spoilers of all time, the man Jacob. He had twelve sons, but he spoiled only one of them, the boy Joseph.

Many of us remember childhood Sunday school lessons that made Joseph a thoroughly heroic figure. He did, indeed, end that way, but he took a circuitous route to that achievement. And the long and sometimes painful route was partly his father's fault.

It's a complicated story. I'll tell you enough of it to give you a background for understanding our eventual hero, Joseph. Jacob fell in love with a beautiful woman, Rachel, and in time was able to gain her hand in marriage. Unfortunately, his father-in-law, who happened also to be his uncle, was a hard-dealing man, so instead of getting Rachel as his wife, Jacob found that he was married to her older sister, Leah. Soon both sisters were married to Jacob, and after that he had two maids who, with the agreement of his wives, also bore him children—after a while, in fact, twelve sons and at least one daughter.

But as you might anticipate, it was a pretty dysfunctional family. With four mothers, twelve sons, a father who adores one of the mothers and seems often to do little more than suffer the services of the other three women—well, hard feelings and fierce competitions are guaranteed to develop. Not surprisingly, the difficulties centered increasingly on Joseph, son of Rachel, the woman Jacob adored.

Some rabbinical writers have reasoned that while Jacob was naturally prejudiced toward this son of Rachel, other elements were also at work. For all his shortcomings (and there were several), Jacob longed for values that lasted. He was in the best sense a spiritual man, one who wanted to commune with God. But the sons who were borne to him by Leah and the two maids seemed anything but spiritual. Reuben, Simeon, and Levi seemed more like their Uncle Esau—the man who sold his birthright for a bowl of soup—than like their father, Jacob. But Joseph was different. When Jacob looked at Joseph, I venture to guess that he saw himself: a man who desired God and goodness. Yes, and Jacob could have reasoned that this son desired such spiritual greatness even more than he had. Joseph probably seemed to have virtues his father had never really achieved. I expect a good many of us hope our children will turn out better than we have. We would like to spare them both our hardships and our mistakes. I think Jacob saw Joseph that way. As for those sons who seemed to have gotten Esau's genetic strain, Jacob must have wondered if in this way he was paying for his sins against that older brother.

When Joseph was seventeen years old, he began tending flocks with the sons of Bilhah and Zilpah, the handmaidens who had become wives to Jacob. Considering the nature of that time and culture, we can rightly judge that these sons were lowest in the family structure. This makes one sense that Joseph's assignment to work with them was a somewhat lowly one. This is strange, first, because one expects Jacob to treat the young man more favorably, and also, that he is so little experienced and advanced at the age of seventeen. In that world, a boy was seen as entering manhood at twelve or thirteen, so that by the age of seventeen a young man was maturing in his work role. One can only imagine that his father had been protecting him—all the more so, no doubt, since his mother had died prematurely, at the birth of Joseph's younger brother, Benjamin.

Joseph may have been young for his age, but he was bright. We read that he brought to his father "a bad report" regarding his older brothers. Rabbinical scholars remind us that "bad report" can be interpreted two ways: bad in the sense that the news it conveyed was bad; or bad in that Joseph was not telling the truth; that is, the report

was wicked in its own right. At the least, the story portrays Joseph as
a talebearer; at the worst, it shows him a liar.

I can't imagine that Jacob ever kept his feelings a secret; this
doesn't seem to have been one of his gifts. Now he put his favoritism
on full display. He gave Joseph a coat that not only glorified his place
in the family but that dramatically put down his ten older brothers.
Some of us remember the description in the King James Version of
the Bible: "a coat of many colors." Our New Revised Standard phrase
is "a long robe with sleeves." Professor Robert Alter translates the
term as "ornamented tunic." I give you these various terms to indicate
that we can't find a perfect translation because we don't know enough
about the fashions of that ancient world to convey the idea to our time
and place. But one thing is sure, the garment made clear that Joseph
was special in his father's eyes, to the point of making it seem that the
older sons as well as Joseph's younger brother were all nearly inci-
dental by comparison.

Then young Joseph made it worse. He had a dream in which he and
his brothers were binding sheaves in the field. Suddenly Joseph's
sheaf stood upright, and all the other sheaves "gathered around it, and
bowed down" (Gen. 37:7). In time the dream came true; one can
assume that the dream came from God. But sometimes we do well
not to tell other people what we think God is telling us, especially if
we seem to be the strategic center of the story. The brothers were irritated, and they told Joseph so.

But while Joseph was bright enough to have extravagant dreams,
he wasn't sensitive enough to know when to keep silent. Even after
his first dream had been so poorly received, Joseph dared to report a
second. In plot, it was like the first, except that this time Joseph's
father and mother also paid him obeisance. Even his father chided
him this time—although his father (who had had his own dream time,
at the place called Bethel) was impressed enough that he "kept the
matter in mind" (Gen. 37:11).

No wonder, then, that when one day the older brothers had a chance
at revenge, they took it. They were pasturing the flocks at an area far
from home. Joseph was now part of management, operating out of the
home office. His father sent him to check up on how his brothers were
doing their work. When the older boys saw him coming, grand coat

and all, they "said to one another, 'Here comes this dreamer. Come now, let us kill him and throw him into one of the pits; then we shall say that a wild animal has devoured him, and we shall see what will become of his dreams" (Gen. 37:19–20).

As it turned out, the brothers followed a different course, else we wouldn't be telling the story now. I dare to say that if the brothers hadn't spared Joseph's life, the whole potential plot of the Old Testament would have collapsed, because it is important to get Jacob's family down to Egypt. One of the brothers, Judah, offered a plan that was both merciful (saving the boy's life) and profitable (selling him to the passing caravan). They then dipped his coat (that despised coat!) in the blood of a goat and reported to their father that Joseph must have been killed by some wild animal. Their despising of Joseph was so great that they felt no regret in bringing devastating grief to their father. Indeed, under the circumstances, their father's grief may have been the cherry on the top of their angry sundae.

So Joseph, stripped to his most basic garments, went bound into Egypt, where he was sold as a slave. Without his executive robe, he looked like a slave. Take the tiara from Miss America and place her, perspiring, at the fast-food window, and she will be just another pretty, tired girl. But rather soon, Joseph demonstrated that his father's faith and his own extravagant dreams might have some substance. In the home into which he was sold as a slave, he began to show that he was perhaps more than a spoiled favorite son. He was handsome (the Bible says so—Gen. 39:6), and I expect he had a good deal of native charm; he wasn't Jacob and Rachel's son for nothing. And he was smart; and beyond all these matters, he was honorable. His owner-employer, Potiphar, was like many an executive: with so many responsibilities, he needed an aide with such intelligence and character that he could be trusted without reservation. Joseph was his man. Potiphar "left all that he had in Joseph's charge" (Gen. 39:6).

If this were a bedtime story for children, it could end right here: the boy who has been mistreated by his older brothers has become a success. Virtue and fortitude have been rewarded. I wonder, even, if at this point Joseph may have trimmed his dreams down to size. Did he begin to think that his future lay in this lovely Egyptian household? After all, he had comfort and security. He was a slave in name only;

in practice he was the aide-de-camp to Captain Potiphar. What do you do with extravagant dreams when you already have rather satisfactory fulfillments?

Obviously we don't know what went through Joseph's mind. It's clear that he had come a very long way from the pampered boy who went off to the pastures in his exquisite coat. And I'm sure his hours in the pit where his brothers threw him while they discussed his future or nonfuture, the humiliation of being sold as chattel property, and the indignation of his early employment in Potiphar's house at the lowest rank must all have helped to form character. Not that such experiences are guaranteed to form character; in some, they simply fester into resentment and self-pity. But Joseph was better than that. His father must have taught him something more than how to stride gracefully in a tailored suit, because he dealt well with adversity. But was he ready for the big leagues of history? Don't you believe it. I submit that he was a work in progress, whether he knew it or not, and one of the greatest chapters in his story was yet to come.

It came painfully, as great chapters sometimes do. Potiphar's wife sought to seduce Joseph. Any novelist has plenty of material here for speculation. The writer of Genesis uses the same Hebrew phrase to describe Joseph (Gen. 39:6) as he used earlier to describe Joseph's mother, Rachel (Gen. 29:17), although our translations use adjectives appropriate to male and female. Clearly, this is a young man with a kind of gentle, seductive attractiveness that asserts itself without his even trying; and being human as we are, perhaps Joseph has learned to augment his natural gifts by a bit of what we call style or flair. And perhaps Potiphar's wife is a neglected woman, the wife of a preoccupied executive. Still more, perhaps she is coming to a place in her life where she has begun to doubt her ability to entice, and who better to restore it than this Hebrew slave. After all, not only is he attractive, he is her property, beholden to her commands.

Joseph tried to reject her invitations graciously. But one day she became so aggressive that when he ran from her presence she grabbed his outer garment, and used it that evening to incriminate Joseph with his employer. So, for a second time in his rather young life, Joseph's garments became the evidence for a lie, and he was reduced again to pathetic nakedness.

This time Joseph was sent to prison. This is worse, even, than the slavery into which his brothers sold him. We have no evidence of a trial; it appears that he was doomed to a sentence that would last until Potiphar, a man of power, chose to recommend his release.

Once again, however, Joseph responded with character. I'm sure more was required this time than before. He had every reason to fret in his cell, with his soul more chained than his limbs. He had done nothing but good, with an unerring eye to his responsibility before both God and his employer, and all it had gotten him was this dank cell. But "the LORD was with him; and whatever he did, the LORD made it prosper" (Gen. 39:23). One day that divine touch seemed to open the door of opportunity. Joseph interpreted dreams for two of his fellow prisoners. When the one was released, as Joseph had predicted he would be, Joseph asked him to appeal his cause before the king. "Yet the chief cupbearer did not remember Joseph, but forgot him" (Gen. 40:23).

Forgot him, in fact, for "two whole years" (Gen. 41:1). Joseph was now thirty years old. He had lived most of his adult life as an alien, in the role of either a slave or a prisoner. But almost as suddenly as he was thrown into a pit thirteen years earlier, he was summoned now to the king's palace. He had time only to shave and change his clothes, though it's quite possible he was still in some sort of prison garb, since jails don't maintain a wardrobe for courtly appearances.

As Joseph demonstrated his extraordinary gifts, the king was quick to provide him with "garments of fine linen"—better, I venture, than his teenage long-sleeved garment, as surely as the tailors of Egypt were more sophisticated than the seamstresses of Israel's semi-wilderness. More than that, the king took his own signet ring and put it on Joseph's hand (Gen. 41:42). Roughly a decade later he was able to save the lives of his father and his brothers and their families; and, yes, his brothers did bow down before him, just as he had dreamed long before.

But the best of the story is this, that Joseph grew into his coat. I don't want to belabor his youthful shortcomings, although I've found that some of the ancient rabbis treated him rather sharply. Reading between the lines, one realizes that he was not only precocious, he was also spoiled and insensitive. Mind you, one would have to have

a very great deal of character to maintain some sort of emotional equilibrium when it's clear every day that the authority you respect
most—your own father—has judged you to be superior to all com-
petition, and then you receive a garment that announces your unique
excellence every time you put it on. Under such circumstances I
would understand if Joseph had become a kind of moral pygmy on
whom his father's garment hung with increasing absurdity.

But instead he grew up. First, in those terrifying opening moments
in the desert pit, where the conversations he overheard suggested that
he might die, despised. Then as he rode, half naked, as a prospective
slave in a traders' caravan. Still more, as a slave, and then as a prisoner, with no reason to hope ever for release or justification.

But in circumstances that were calculated to diminish Joseph, he
grew. So when his father saw him, Joseph now turning forty, Jacob
could see, by the cut of Joseph's character, that he had been right in
ordering him that coat of grandeur. Premature, mind you, but right.

Joseph's coat was like every baptismal gown, every cute little out-
fit worn by a child brought to the altar of the church. When we
announce that this child is now part of the kingdom of heaven, in fact
the statement is premature. But in truth, it is right. All we need pray
is that the child will grow up to fit the garment. That's the best part
of the Joseph story: in time, through pain and character, he grew into
his coat.

Chapter 4

The Man Moses

Scripture Reading: Exodus 2:1–22

*M*oses has been part of my life since before kindergarten. My childhood book of Bible stories began Moses' story with an endearing picture of a baby floating among the reeds of the Nile River's bank, and continued on into some rather horrendous pictures of the plagues that came on Egypt after Moses became Israel's leader. But his greatest attraction for me has come in more recent years. I like the fact that, as the book of Exodus tells it, his career didn't really begin to develop until he was eighty years old. This fascinates me. Mind you, I began preaching when I was still in my teens and I've had many good years since then. But some of the best things that have happened to me have come in later years. So when I see how Moses' life took off around his eightieth birthday (Exod. 7:7), I tell myself that the excitement in my life has just begun.

I owe my chapter title to the fine Hebrew scholar Robert Alter. He reminds us that Moses is "alone among biblical characters" in being given the "oddly generic epithet, 'the man Moses.'" Alter suggests that the title may be meant to remind us that while Moses is indeed one who forges a nation and is "prince of prophets," he is nevertheless "not an absolutely unique figure but a man like other men."[1] That, too, is a good reason for him to be in this little book. He's a giant among men, no doubt about that, but he wouldn't be so worth knowing if he were entirely out of our reach. We may have to gasp at times when we breathe at his altitude, but the air is not so rare that we can't exist there.

As you may remember, he was born at a bad time. But as Charles Dickens advised us, the best of times and the worst of times have a way of coexisting. I said a moment ago that Moses was a giant among men. I doubt that such a towering personality can develop in good times or even in ordinary times. Greatness probably needs a dark stage of near despair if it is to reach its potential.

Moses' people, the children of Israel, had been slaves for more than three centuries by the time he was born. This means there was no one in Israel with a living definition for freedom—nor, for that matter, did they have a definition for dignity, independence, or self-worth. I recall that there were some in the early nineteenth century in America who said that it took four generations to make a gentleman; that is, that some instincts have to be bred into one over a long period. I wonder how many generations it takes to make a person a slave? I have a theological prejudice about this. I believe God has invested a measure of divinity in us humans that makes it essentially impossible to extinguish our sense of worth. People and governments and circumstances can bring the flame to ashes, but if a right person or a right idea blows on those ashes, the fire will spring up again. You and I are made of too good stuff for us to acquiesce completely to denigration.

So it is that when Moses was born, his parents managed to spare his life. At that time Israel's slaves were under orders to throw every newborn male child into the Nile River, thus minimizing the possibility of revolt by the slaves, or of their joining forces with some invading nation. But when Moses was born, his mother "saw that he was a fine baby" so she hid him for three months. "A fine baby." It's a fascinating phrase. From what I've been able to observe, nearly all parents thinks their newborn is a "fine baby." Obviously more was at stake here; this mother saw something unique in this child—let's call it a sense of destiny. So, at the peril of her whole household, she preserved the baby for three months, until it was no longer possible to conceal him. Then, in a perverse way, she followed the royal command to take the baby to the Nile; but instead of throwing him in, she placed him in a tiny papyrus basket, "among the reeds on the bank of the river" (Exod. 2:2–3).

There the baby was discovered by, of all people, the daughter of Pharaoh. The woman's maternal instincts locked in. She took pity on the crying infant, and raised him as her own son. Thus it was that Moses received a royal education, including as a New Testament writer said, "the treasures of Egypt" (Heb. 11:26). He enjoyed this privileged life until he was forty years old, when something extraordinary happened. The story I've told thus far has had several miracles: that the mother would sense this child's uniqueness; that his life would be spared by Pharaoh's daughter; that his own mother would be able to nurse him and influence his earliest life; and that Pharaoh's daughter would raise him as her own son. Now we're about to see an even greater miracle.

One day, "after Moses had grown up," he went out where his biological people the Israelites were. He saw an Egyptian "beating a Hebrew, one of his kinsfolk" (Exod. 2:11). Sure no one could see what he was doing, Moses killed the Egyptian and hid his body. Here was a miracle of considerable dimension: that Moses would feel his ethnic ties after spending comfortable formative years in Pharaoh's court, and that those ties would be so strong that he would endanger his standing and his future to express his allegiance to his birth people.

This was one of Moses' highest moments. He had nothing to gain and everything to lose by affiliating himself with the Hebrews. The folk saying insists that "blood is thicker than water." Moses' story says that blood is also thicker than gold, at least for some people. Am I justifying the murder Moses committed? By no means. Indeed, while referring to this incident as one of Moses' highest moments, I can also say that it is one of his lowest. Moses had the right intentions, but he fulfilled them the wrong way. Once again someone is going to challenge me: without this murder Moses would never have been driven from Egypt and might never, therefore, have delivered the Israelites from their slavery, so the murder must have been in the purposes of God. I doubt it. I don't associate the will of God with murder. But I marvel that God can take the misshapen pieces of our earnestness and eventually make something worthwhile of them. As I look through the Scriptures and church history—and indeed, even as I look carefully at my own life—I think that perhaps God does as much with our errors as with our wisdom. I can't prove this, of course, but I can find a good many dramatic case histories. And I'm quite sure it was the case in this particular instance, both in its good intentions and in God's use of human anger and ineptness.

We see this because, by the murder, Moses was made a fugitive.

He fled to the land of Midian, where he married a daughter of the priest of Midian, and for the next third of his life he tended sheep. In my youth there was a popular saying among churches that were served by new seminary graduates: "It takes three years for a person to get through seminary and five years to get over it." I suspect that Moses needed the forty years of sheep tending to get over forty years in Pharaoh's court. We're told later that "the man Moses was very humble, more so than anyone else on the face of the earth" (Num. 12:3). He didn't gain his humility as Pharaoh's grandson; this came as part of his postgraduate work in the deserts of Midian.

One day in that desert, Moses encountered God. I don't know that this was the first time Moses experienced God in a memorable way. I am inclined to feel that the seeds of his faith were planted by his mother in the gentle days as "the child grew up," before "she brought him to Pharaoh's daughter" (Exod. 2:10). I believe in the importance of climactic religious experiences of the kind we commemorate in persons like Augustine, Blaise Pascal, John Wesley, or Thomas Merton—to say nothing of thousands of others of us whose stories never merit mention in books or on plaques. But I suspect virtually every such decisive experience is preceded and followed by lesser but nevertheless shaping moments.

At any rate, one day Moses met God in a no-turning-back moment, in a bush that burned but was not consumed. But it was not one of Moses' better hours. However much he was moved when God said, "I have observed the misery of my people . . . ; I have heard their cry. . . . I know their sufferings, and I have come down to deliver them," I doubt that he was ready for the divine conclusion: "So come, I will send you to Pharaoh to bring my people, the Israelites, out of Egypt" (Exod. 3:7–8, 10). Moses stubbornly resisted God's call, insisting finally that he was too "slow of speech and slow of tongue" to approach Pharaoh—and this after he had used his speech and tongue very vigorously in contending with God. Finally, when assured by God that his brother Aaron could become his spokesman, Moses accepted his call reluctantly. I repeat, the man Moses had better hours.

But who am I to judge? Somehow herding sheep can seem very attractive when you're asked to challenge a king on behalf of a small nation of slaves.

Once he accepted this challenge, Moses performed magnificently. The writer of Exodus puts the transition with direct, poignant power: "So Moses took his wife and his sons, put them on a donkey and went back to the land of Egypt; and Moses carried the staff of God in his hand" (Exod. 4:20). His brother Aaron met him in the wilderness, and together they met with the elders of Israel. One wonders how a people who had lived in slavery for four centuries still managed to keep an underground societal structure; we learn something about the indomitable strength of the human spirit when we see people insisting on an order of their own when the powers that control them deny them any significance.

But very shortly Moses and Aaron learned that they were facing not one enemy, but two, and that the intransigence of Pharaoh was no worse than the impatience of their fellow Israelites. Each time Pharaoh rejected their propositions or made commitments then broke them, the two brothers had to rally the spirits of their kin, because each time their negotiations with Pharaoh failed, the condition of the slaves grew more hopeless. As the story unfolds in the book of Exodus, you notice an amusing incongruity. Although Moses had insisted, "Since I am a poor speaker, why would Pharaoh listen to me?" and although God agreed for Aaron to speak on Moses' behalf, it doesn't work out that way. Again and again it is Moses who challenges Pharaoh, while his brother Aaron handles the implementation of miracles. And as the story builds to a climax the writer tells us, "Moreover, Moses himself was a man of great importance in the land of Egypt, in the sight of Pharaoh's officials and in the sight of the people" (Exod. 11:3). That doesn't sound like the kind of bumbling presenter Moses had declared himself to be.

Have no doubt about it, the man Moses is an extraordinary personality. Raised in the privileges of a king's household and educated to maintain and enjoy those privileges, he chooses one day to step out of the security of his position long enough to see the condition of his native people. There, seemingly from nowhere, the passion of a reformer strikes him with such force that he kills a man in defense of an unknown slave. With that, the prince becomes a fugitive, and the fugitive becomes a shepherd. This long period was all gain. From what we learn later about Moses' father-in-law, Jethro, I'm confident

Moses learned a very great deal in long evening conversations with this man. Tending sheep prepared Moses to lead a generally helpless, easily dispirited people. And the desert gave him time to think. In all his appearances before Pharaoh and then with his own people, and in the years that followed as the Israelites headed fretfully and circuitously to their promised land, Moses drew on the training of his palace tutors, the wisdom of his father-in-law, the rugged strength of the desert, and the memory of a burning bush.

So the people escaped Egypt, marched through the Red Sea, and headed into the wilderness that led to the land that God had promised to them. Moses didn't coin the phrase, but he quickly learned that armies do indeed march on their stomachs, and Moses' army—along with their wives and children and sisters and parents—had a great many stomachs for the marching. This led to trouble. The people became impatient with their diet, a kind of pastry (I use the word loosely) that awaited them on the ground each morning. Apparently this food (they called it "manna," which actually meant, "What is it?") contained all the necessary elements, because it met their needs for roughly forty years. But it lacked variety, and we humans have sought variety ever since Eve and Adam reached for that fruit in the garden of Eden. Moses found himself in the uniquely difficult position of a table server whose customers don't like the plate set before them and whose chef says, "That's what I'm serving today, like it or not." Under the circumstances Moses the man didn't always keep his cool, but as I see it, he did remarkably well.

The high point of Moses' career, it seems to me, was when he pleaded the case of his nation before God. It happened like this: Moses was on Mount Sinai for forty days, receiving the Law. This proved a bit long for his people, so they asked his brother, Aaron, to make gods for them. The God Moses talked about had always been invisible, and now that Moses was also invisible, the people wanted something a little more tangible, like the gods the Egyptians worshiped. Aaron cooperated. When Moses came down from the mountain, "the people were running wild (for Aaron had let them run wild, to the derision of their enemies)" (Exod. 32:25). Moses restored order, though at a bloody price. Then he returned to do business with God. There he threw down a remarkable gauntlet. "Alas, this people has sinned a great sin; they have made for themselves gods of gold. But now, if you will only forgive their sin—but if not, blot me out of the book that you have written" (Exod. 32:31–32).

Mark this down as one of the most momentous events of human history. I believe Moses was saying several things. For one, that he loved this people more than he loved his own life; indeed, in a peculiar sense, more than he loved God. Scholars would probably argue whether or not Moses believed in a life beyond the grave, but he was surely saying that he was casting his lot with the fate of the people rather than with God. If you love me, he seemed to be telling God, you'll have to love these people too. Still more, Moses was telling God that if God was going to break off his relationship with Israel for what they had done, he didn't really care to continue his own relationship with God. God replied that he would decide for himself who was in the book and who was blotted out, while making clear that some judgment would fall. But Israel remained God's chosen people.

The Bible is a remarkable book. It dares to give us a story in which God comes near seeming the villain, and a mere human being is made heroic by insisting that God define the divine character. Indeed, this human seems to say, "If you don't measure up to a standard that one of your own creatures sees as right, I don't want to work with you any longer"; and God, blessed be the Name, honors his upstart first lieutenant. It's quite a story.

Moses had some hard days after that. His most disappointing came in a moment of pique. You hate to see a great soul stumble on a pebble, but I've observed that pebbles get us more often than mountains. On one of those occasions, when the Israelites were without water, God instructed Moses as to how he should get an abundant supply. Instead, irritated with his people, he disobeyed God and did it his own way. The water came, but God told Moses he would never get to enter the land of promise toward which he was leading his people. He was able finally to see it from a mountaintop, but was never to enter it. Nevertheless, the biographer in Deuteronomy reported that God himself saw to Moses' burial, and that he "was one hundred twenty years old when he died; his sight was unimpaired and his vigor had not abated" (Deut. 34:7).

Professor Alter was right in reminding us of the uniqueness of "the man Moses." He was altogether human. But he was quite a man.

Chapter 5

A Man after God's Own Heart

Scripture Reading: 1 Samuel 16:1–12

*E*veryone is special to God, but some are especially special. I don't mean this as an evidence of favoritism on God's part; I think, rather, it's that some people make it easier for God to know them. Friendship with God is in many ways like friendship between humans. It takes two to make a really good friendship happen. The persons who become very special to God aren't necessarily the most talented, the most naturally attractive, or the most consistent in conduct. It's just that they pursue the friendship more passionately. And sometimes the qualities in the divine-human friendship are as unlikely as in the friendships some of us enjoy, even as we admit that they aren't altogether logical.

I'm thinking just now of a person called David. He lived roughly three thousand years ago, but he's the reason that people around the world still choose to call their sons David. Mind you, they may name their son after a family member or a friend, but trace it back and back and back, and it will lead you to this David. Eventually he was *King* David, and although the country he ruled was not big by any standard, he is one of the most famous kings in human history. Name any ancient king or ruler, or even a fairly modern one—King Nebuchadnezzar from long ago, or Alexander the Great, or Julius Caesar, or Henry the Eighth, or Richard the Lion-Hearted—name your king and I think I can prove that King David is better known. On any day of the week, more people will read one of the poems attributed to David (because he was a poet, as well as a king) than will read Caesar's "Gallic Wars" in all of a year or all of a decade. A modern nation,

Israel, celebrates the memory of King David by using his star as the symbol on its flag. We have no sure idea of what David looked like, but I venture the guess that there are more artistic interpretations of him, in paintings and sculpture, than any three other kings or rulers combined.

But none of this is the best thing about King David. Here is what matters: the Bible says of him that he was "a man after [God's] own heart."

So let me tell you his story. Israel, the little nation in which David grew up, suffered a variety of humiliations for several centuries after establishing itself as an independent people in the days of Moses and Joshua. I think the people suffered a kind of inferiority complex as a nation, because for a long time they didn't have the kind of political structure that other nations had. They were told that God was their King, and that the various military and civic persons who led them were doing so under God's command. Eventually the people decided that what they really needed was to have a king, like the nations around them. This would help their national ego as they related to their neighboring peoples.

So they got a king, a man named Saul, and for a while he did a really admirable job. But then he got carried away with his own importance. This is a common failing of kings, emperors, plastic surgeons, and taxicab drivers, not to mention a few professors. Saul got it bad, so that one day God said, "I've had enough," and God asked his faithful prophet, Samuel, to anoint a new king. Mind you, this new king wouldn't take over the throne immediately, but he would be in the wings, ready to move center stage when the time came.

God told Samuel that this new king would be found in the household of Jesse, a farmer who got his mail at the Bethlehem post office. So Samuel went to Jesse's home. Immediately, Samuel was impressed with Eliab, the oldest son. He struck a remarkable figure. But God rebuked Samuel's taste. "Do not look on his appearance," God said, "or on the height of his stature, because I have rejected him; for the LORD does not see as mortals see; they look on the outward appearance, but the LORD looks on the heart" (1 Sam. 16:7).

There you have it. God looks at things from a very different vantage point. We look at the outward appearances. We really do, you know. Men don't set out at age twelve or thirteen to get a really lovely heart. We try, if anything, to get good abs, and a neck like a bull. Later we try to get lots of hair; and if we can't get lots of it, we decide to shave off what we have. We just worry a lot about how we look. I have no right to speak for women, but if one can learn from television commercials (and I regret that one can), women are being sold on several things besides a beautiful heart. Mind you, some women and a few men, too, get a great heart, but it doesn't usually come easily. Yet this is what God looks for. And pretty clearly this has something to do with one's being a person after God's own heart.

So, as we see in David's story, God looks beneath the surface, beneath the cosmetics of life, the clothing, the touched-up publicity photos. God looks at the heart.

Well, Samuel examined seven outstanding young men, and God kept saying, "Nope." This was very discouraging, because this was all the sons Jesse had brought. Samuel must have begun thinking he had come to the wrong farm, or that perhaps there was another Jesse on the other side of Bethlehem. But Samuel was persistent. "Are all your sons here?" he asked. And Jesse confessed that there was, in fact, another, "the youngest, but he is keeping the sheep" (1 Sam. 16:11).

Do you wonder how Jesse failed to mention him? We read shortly that he was "ruddy" (you would be too, if you stood in the Middle Eastern sun all day), and that he had "beautiful eyes," and that he "was handsome." But he was tending sheep. I sense (and here, I'm getting speculative) that there's something significant in the numbers. Jesse had seven sons, and then he had David. In Israel, seven was the number of completeness—as in seven days in a week, and seven golden lampstands in the temple. After Jesse and his wife had seven sons, I suspect they said, "That's it. This is perfect, it's complete. We have seven sons." I think his wife, especially, said something like that. But then along came David. He was an afterthought. Or more correctly, he came without thought. Anyway, he was tending the sheep.

But Samuel asked that he be brought in, and when he appeared, God said to Samuel, "Rise and anoint him; for this is the one" (1 Sam. 16:12). And that day David was anointed king of Israel. It would be years before he came to the throne, years of testing, of danger, of victories, of defeat and pain. But the issue was settled that day, when Samuel anointed the shepherd boy. He was going to be king.

His record, from that time forward, was actually quite mixed. He was the noblest of men at times, the most admirable figure. But he was also given to rambunctious, dangerous, self-destructive conduct. With all of that, he was a born leader. When he heard that Israel and Israel's God were being ridiculed by a pagan giant, he challenged the giant. You know the story. The shepherd boy, the talented musician who could soothe the troubled breast by playing his harp, he slew the pride of the Philistines. That day, David won the hearts of the people, and he struck fear into the heart of Saul, the king. Saul might wear the crown and sit on the throne, but this shepherd boy from Bethlehem was in the hearts of the people. And Saul didn't know it, but David was also in the heart of God.

Eventually, David had to run for his life. He spent several years on the run, fleeing from the king who was out to destroy him. Twice, David had Saul's life in the very palm of his hand, and twice he refused to strike the death blow. He could not, he said, because Saul was God's anointed. David believed in the purposes of God. And he believed so thoroughly in what had happened years before, when Samuel anointed him to be king, that he didn't think it would be right for him to take the throne on his own. He believed that if God wanted him to be king, God would bring it off without questionable help from David.

At one point during those years of exile, David almost killed a man out of simple, self-centered anger, but a wise woman kept him from it. She told him that he would be ashamed someday if he followed his instincts and killed the man. Fortunately, David believed her. I think it helped that she was also beautiful. David, like most men, found it easy to believe beautiful women. That was one of his weaknesses, but in this particular instance, he was right.

Eventually, David came to the throne. He was an effective king, just as he had been a persuasive leader in the little band he had gathered about him in earlier years. People believed in him, trusted him, and loved him. He was not a perfect man, but he showed great capacity for love—for loving God and loving people. With all of his great skills—poet, musician, warrior, administrator—I believe David's greatest skill was this, his capacity to love. I suspect that this was also his greatest peril. This is how he got into trouble numbers of times, not only in the infamous incident with Bathsheba, but also in relationships within his own family, especially with his son, Absalom. There is a lesson here, of course: the quality that is our greatest strength is usually also our greatest danger.

But I repeat, here was the best of David: he was willing to dare to love. He loved his people, his family, his nation, and most of all his God. When we read that David was a man after God's own heart, remember that he was a person who knew how to *love*.

This is a gift within the reach of every one of us. I'm sure it's easier for some than for others. I'm sure, too, that some of us have been hurt by loving, so that we are very cautious about loving again. It's altogether possible that some of us feel that way about God. We've loved God and trusted God, but we aren't sure God has treated us fairly in return. Well, that's the hazard of loving: loving always is a fearful gamble. That's because loving is an expression of faith. And that's the biggest gift we can offer to another person or to God: faith that expresses itself in love.

As the rest of David's story unfolds, you see wonderful moments and dreadful ones. He does noble things and shameful things, wise and stupid, forgiving and vengeful. But in total, he is a person after God's own heart. So much so that when you continue reading in the books of Kings and Chronicles—the long history of the various kings that followed David to the throne—an interesting phrase appears again and again. Generations after David is gone, the historian will write of numerous kings a sentence that will go like this: "So and so was a great king; he followed God with all of his heart, like his father David." Or a sentence like this: "So and so was a great king, but he did not follow God with all of his heart, like his father David."

But this description of David's loyalty to God needs some thoughtful defining. As we have already noticed, David was far from a perfect human being. He did some quite evil and immoral things. So what was the quality in his character and conduct that redeemed his lapses of character?

Just this: David knew how to repent. He knew how to admit he was wrong, to be sorry for it, and to change his ways.

For many years I have been impressed by the double tragedy of the Eden story, that succinct, stirring report of what we sometimes call "the first sin." I came to feel that though the obvious point of the story is the rupture of Adam and Eve's relationship with God, the second tragedy in the story is in its own way equally crucial. This is because, challenged by God regarding their conduct, Adam and Eve refused to face themselves; Adam blamed Eve for his transgression, and Eve blamed the serpent. If they had acknowledged their fault, there would have been a foundation on which to begin a new life. That is to say, it's bad enough to sin, but it is even worse to ignore or deny the sin or to excuse our wrongheadedness. It is in the acknowledging of our need that we begin the process of restoration.

David was good at that. When the prophet Nathan confronted him after his sin with Bathsheba, David made no attempt to excuse himself or to use his kingly prerogatives; he repented with an almost ferocious intensity. So, too, late in his career, when in arrogance he took a census of the people. When he realized the enormity of his wrongdoing—and was reminded of it again by someone whose judgment he could easily have dismissed—he took full responsibility, and grieved for the pain he had given his nation: "I alone have sinned, and I alone have done wickedly; but these sheep, what have they done? Let your hand, I pray, be against me and against my father's house" (2 Sam. 24:17). To err may indeed be human, and to forgive, divine; but to face up to ourselves and to acknowledge that we have erred— ah, that is a right step toward true holiness. In this quality, David's spiritual nobility is magnificent.

David became the measuring stick for all the kings that followed him. No wonder, then, that he is the symbol on Israel's flag still today. And see what it was that made him great. He conquered Goliath and saved Israel's national pride, he picked up the pieces after the death of King Saul and eventually reunited the people, he led his nation's armies in victory after victory, never really knowing the taste of defeat, and he ruled with justice and mercy.

But it is for none of these that he is uniquely remembered. When the biblical historians look back on his reign, they do not praise his military triumphs, his administrative genius, or the buildings he erected in the capital city. It is his heart. He followed God with all his heart.

I repeat: this is an ability within the reach of every human being.

We are capable of loving. We are capable of taking the risk: the risk of faith that dares to love.

When Jesus was asked to sum up the law, he said that it all hung on two things: love the Lord our God with all our being, and love our neighbor as ourselves. King David did just this, even if imperfectly. When he fell short, he repented of it and tried again. But he dared to love. And because he did, the Scriptures say of him this extraordinary thing, that David was a man after God's own heart.

I don't think there's an easy formula here. There are no "seven steps to becoming a loving person." I suspect it helps if we can start early, but I've known some remarkable instances of individuals whose upbringing was so lacking in love that they hardly knew how to recognize love, let alone exercise it, yet in time they became great lovers. I'm sure, too, that some folks have a head start because they seem to come from a family line where love is strong. But such a heritage is neither a requirement nor a guarantee.

I believe that love, like such other virtues as faith and kindness and patience, comes by intention—that is, by dedicating ourselves to its pursuit. On the whole, we generally get from this life, in one measure or another, what we earnestly go after.

That's why, when I read David's story, I have hope for myself and for you too. I don't think this ruddy farm boy had a huge edge on us. He simply exercised his hunger for God more than his desire for a great many other things; and when he missed the way, he admitted it, repented, and changed. We can too. We can delight the heart of God, by David's simple, self-demanding example.

Chapter 6

My Friend, Elijah

Scripture Reading: 1 Kings 19:1–12

I have always liked Elijah. He has fascinated me from the first time I met him while reading the Bible through as an eleven-year-old. I was captured at first by his heroics: anybody who could challenge kings and queens and be unafraid when outnumbered hundreds to one was pretty dazzling for a boy with a modest stock of courage.

But I came to a new level of affection for Elijah and of understanding his personality through a friendship that blessed me from high school until almost the present time—that is, until this friend's death. When I saw this friend I saw Elijah, and when I read of Elijah I saw my friend. I suspect that at times all of us see ourselves or people we know in biblical characters, just as we say of a character in a novel or in a television sitcom, "She reminds me of your sister Amber." On the whole, it's probably good when we make such a biblical connection; it takes the Bible personalities out of stained glass so that we can see them as real human beings, as of course they were. I'm not encouraging you to build some sort of doctrine around such imaginary resemblances, I'm simply saying that when we relate to a character in the Bible as we might to one in a novel or a movie, we're likely to make association with that character, and that on the whole we have a better feeling for the Bible when we do so.

So, as I started to say, while I have always liked Elijah, I came to feel closer to him as I saw similarities between him and my cherished friend. I think my lifelong friend was born in a crisis, because he always lived in one. I doubt that one could be as crisis-ridden as he was unless one had a head start. Through our high school days I talked with him about my faith with a directness that I'm afraid I've lost in my adult years; and, partly as a result of those conversations, my friend became a Christian soon after we graduated from high school.

I must tell you, however, that becoming a Christian didn't eliminate my friend's crisis-inclination. It seemed, rather, to baptize it. This helped me learn early that conversion doesn't necessarily change our personality type. But, given a fair chance, a true conversion equips us to deal with what we are. That's quite a victory, as my friend came to realize.

Through my years of reading the Bible I have come to realize that we don't need to feel guilty about our personality types. Now, that doesn't mean we should happily acquiesce to unpleasant shortcomings; Christians ought, above all people, to be committed to growing up. If there is any insight to be read into the phrase "born again," it is the expectation that we will grow. Birth is not an end in itself, whether the birth is physical or spiritual. The purpose of being born is to move on to maturity. But that maturation process differs as greatly as the personalities in whom it operates.

For my friend and for the prophet Elijah, crisis was the determining life pattern. It was at times the instrument through which God worked miracles, and at other times the catalyst for near disaster. Now understand: all of us deal with crises now and again, some of us more and some of us less. Life is made that way. But for some people the crises are more frequent, more pervasive, and much more dramatic. If crises could be charted by some sort of medical graph, the Elijah type would need extended lows and highs to carry the story.

For Elijah, life was a rough road. He was a person of vigorous and tempestuous moods. In a winning streak, he was magnificent. When he was losing, he descended to the pits.

We know nothing about his origins except that he came from the area of Tishbe in Gilead. Listen; here's the way the Bible introduces him to us: "Now Elijah the Tishbite, of Tishbe in Gilead, said to [King] Ahab, 'As the LORD the God of Israel lives, before whom I stand, there shall be neither dew nor rain these years, except by my word'" (1 Kings 17:1).

Just like that! The Bible doesn't tell us how old Elijah was, who his parents were, whether he was married or single (though he has all the marks of a thoroughgoing loner), or what he was doing before that day when he suddenly intruded on the court of King Ahab and Queen Jezebel. He burst on the scene like a visitor from another planet. And it was no quiet entrance. He simply announced that there would be no more rain until he authorized it. Nor did he apologize about his source of authority: "As the LORD the God of Israel lives, *before whom I stand*" (emphasis added). This was a way of telling the king, "You have no jurisdiction over me. I am under the authority of another emperor."

It appears that Elijah didn't wait long for a reaction to this sermon; there was no greeting folks at the door or other such social niceties. He left as abruptly as he had arrived, with instructions from God to hide in an area east of the Jordan River. You get the feeling that God accommodated the divine style to the style of the messenger. Elijah learned that he would drink water from a wadi—that is, the little channel of a watercourse that is dry except in rainy seasons. That isn't a very promising provision when you've just predicted a sustained drought. Elijah's food was to be delivered by ravens. Ravens are scavenger birds; the biblical dietary laws considered them unclean. If you're the kind of person who hopes your server at the restaurant has manicured nails, you would be uncomfortable with raven service. But I repeat, God seems to have adjusted the food and water service to the style of the messenger, Elijah.

So the raven brought bread and meat in the morning and bread and meat in the evening. One wonders where the ravens got their meat, but it isn't polite to raise that question, even though it helps us empathize with Elijah. Eventually, as you might have expected, the water in the wadi ran out. Elijah was then directed to a widow in Zarephath, who was to take care of him. If food delivered by ravens happened to trouble Elijah's sense of cleanliness, this new arrangement must surely have offended his sense of manliness and independence.

After three years of drought—years when Elijah remained in hiding—he was instructed to appear again before King Ahab. Once again it was a tempestuous moment. The king said, "Is it you, you troubler of Israel?" and Elijah replied, "Troubler? *You're* the troubler!" This isn't recommended in the Dale Carnegie training as a way to win friends and influence kings. But, as I've already said, Elijah was a personality inclined to crisis. I think the prophet Jeremiah might have come to Ahab with tears in his eyes; Elijah came with a dismissive toss of the head and a throwing down of the gauntlet. Some would have been solicitous in dealing with the king, reasoning that a conciliatory approach might soften his heart. But not Elijah. He seemed bent on trouble.

Perhaps you know what happened next. The story is one of the most famous in all of the Old Testament. One of its scenes practically begs for Cecil B. DeMille to return and put it on the screen. Elijah set himself against the 450 prophets of Baal and the 400 prophets of Asherah, then challenged all the people who had come for this World Series of faith to stop halting between two opinions. There was nothing seeker-sensitive about Elijah's approach. He didn't care about the feelings of his audience—his challenge rasped against the tentativeness that marked the attitudes of the people. For Elijah the issue was simple: it was his duty to deliver the message and theirs to respond, and let the devil take the hindmost.

You see what I mean? Elijah loved a crisis. Crises were his food, night and day. Season them however you will, just give Elijah a crisis. In any event, he won a great victory for God that day. The false prophets were routed and Elijah stood in lonely, victorious splendor. Then, to add more luster to the day, Elijah dared to promise King Ahab that God would send rain. After three years of gasping drought, there would be plentiful, magnificent rain.

Life at this moment was at a zenith for the prophet. And if King Ahab had been the only issue, life would probably have continued to be nothing but triumphs. But Ahab had a wife, Queen Jezebel, and she was easily the powerhouse in the family. When she heard what Elijah had done to her prophets, she vowed she would have his life within twenty-four hours.

At first thought, you may reason that Elijah will handle this threat with the back of his hand. After all, he has already disposed of Jezebel's religious leadership. But if you know Elijah's personality, you know that it may work just the other way. Someone who is capable of rising to such heights of ecstasy is also susceptible to poignant plunges into despair. Life with Elijah was never tedious. It seems almost certain that Elijah wasn't married, and that's a mercy, because any woman who might have been married to him would have had an exhausting assignment. Mind you, she would never have been bored, but she might have longed for an occasional vacation.

Elijah went a day's journey into the wilderness, where he sat down under "a solitary broom tree" (1 Kings 19:4). The broom tree isn't really a tree at all, it's just a good-sized bush. But sometimes it grows as high as ten feet, and in the Middle Eastern desert it's as good a source of shade as you're likely to find. Agreed, it wasn't much, but it was all Elijah had.

And in that nearly desolate place, God visited Elijah. I never cease marveling at the humility of God, the quality that causes God to pursue us when we are in inhospitable places. In my days as a pastor I sometimes reminded myself of this aspect of the divine character, in those instances when I visited people in settings where I would rather not have been. My pastoral assignments were generally in pleasant places, and yet my work took me often enough to places that Frank Mason North described as "haunts of wretchedness and need, / On shadowed thresholds dark with fears."[1] When natural repugnance made me want to draw back, I remembered that the God I profess to serve follows our repugnant human trail into the limits of desolation.

Under the broom tree, Elijah asked God that he might die. "It is enough; now, O LORD, take away my life, for I am no better than my ancestors" (1 Kings 19:4). With that, Elijah fell asleep. I've always seen this sleep as a gift from God; when we are in the sloughs of despond—which was surely Elijah's setting—we sometimes need nothing so much as a good, long nap. God awakened the prophet and gave him food. Elijah lay down again, and once more God touched him and gave him still more food. In the strength of that food, Elijah traveled for forty days and forty nights, to Mount Horeb. The time of his journey is significant. For the Hebrews, who saw significance in particular numbers, forty was the number of trial, judgment, or testing. I'm sure that forty-day trip was a trying time.

But in spite of all the wonderful evidence of God's care, Elijah still wasn't ready to make a declaration of faith. He moved into a cave. On the one hand, this can be seen as a pragmatic act; where better to hide away than in a cave? But it was also, symbolically, an act shrouded in darkness. As the late, great preacher Ralph W. Sockman once said,

"Elijah was in the cave mood," so that "both his mind and his heart had gone into hiding. He was still free from Ahab and Jezebel, but he was a prisoner of himself."[2] Of all the bad neighborhoods in which one might live, none is so subtle and so consuming as that one where we become prisoners of ourselves. I'm very sure that some people whose physical address is enviable may nevertheless be living in a cave, a cave of their own making.

God addressed a question to Elijah: "What are you doing here?" Obviously, God wasn't trying to learn Elijah's address—he was challenging Elijah to acknowledge it. But Elijah was not intimidated by God. Now here is a fascinating human anomaly. Elijah was frightened of Jezebel—a powerful personality, mind you, but a pretty minor character as history writes its total—but he confronts God without hesitation. Is this because God, the unseen, wasn't as real to Elijah as Jezebel, the seen? Or is it because Elijah knew he could expect a just hearing from God? Or was it, perhaps, that Elijah's friendship with God was of such proportions that he dared to be utterly candid with God? Whatever, Elijah dared to let God know how he felt.

"I have been zealous for you," Elijah announced, "and I'm the only one." Of course, there's self-pity in Elijah's complaint, but most of us in our moments of honesty understand the tone of voice. God answered with a series of manifestations: a great wind, an earthquake, a fire, and a still, small voice. Again, God asked Elijah what he was doing in this place. Elijah still wasn't intimidated, or even impressed. He had his excuse and he was sticking by it: I've been loyal to you (see how loyal!) and I'm the only one. To which God answered (I paraphrase): "Shape up! I have work for you to do. And just incidentally, you aren't as alone as you like to think. There are still seven thousand who haven't bowed the knee to Baal."

There's still more to Elijah's story, but by now you get the point. Everybody who tries to walk with God has some trials along the way, and some victories too. But Elijah was one of those persons who got his experiences in Technicolor. Life was a roller coaster for him.

I don't think Elijah was an easy fellow to do business with. When the younger prophet, Elisha, went into apprenticeship with him, I think he discovered as much. But between you and me, if you had talked with Elijah, I think he might have said that God wasn't easy to do business with either. At least that's the report Elijah would have given if you had visited him at the broom tree, or at his cave.

In truth, our perception of God is often rather much a reflection of who and what we are, including the who and what of a given time. But know this for sure: our personalities, whatever they may be— however mercurial, however at times indefensible—are no mystery to God and no match for God's grace. Are you as quiet as Isaac? God understands. Are you as solid as Andrew? God can handle that too. Or are you as emotional and as inclined to highs and lows as Elijah? If so, God understands, and God seems ready patiently to cope with your personality. I suspect that many of Elijah's problems and moods were of his own making. This is true not only of a tempestuous soul like Elijah or my lifelong friend, but of each one of us. I have discovered (no great wisdom here!) that most of my troubles are of my own making, and most of the time when I find myself in some cave it's because I have deliberately, if unwittingly, walked into it. But no human personality is beyond God's ken, or God's grace, either.

As a matter of fact, a New Testament writer, James, seems in a peculiar way to endorse Elijah's unpredictable personality. In his attempt to explain the power of prayer and of faith, the apostolic writer says, "The prayer of the righteous is powerful and effective" (James 5:16). Then, to illustrate his point, he chooses Elijah as his example. But he does so in a fascinating way. As William Barclay puts it in his translation, "Elijah was a man every bit as human as we are" (James 5:17). Yet it was through this man that rain was stopped, then started again, and the spiritual integrity of the nation restored.

James could have described Elijah in any number of ways—as a person of courage, as a man who held to his cause, or as a prophet who made kings quake. Instead he chose to make quiet reference to his mercurial character: "a man every bit as human as we are." I don't see that as an endorsement of roller-coaster character. But I do see it as testimony that God can use the stuff of which we're made, however unseemly at times it may be.

No wonder I've always liked Elijah.

Chapter 7

"Stubborn Ounces"

Scripture Reading: Amos 7:10–17

*C*onventional wisdom teaches us to choose our battles carefully. Arrange a team's schedule so that at best it has a chance of winning its share of games, and at worst its defeats won't be too humiliating. This is good sense. Our Lord himself advised as much on an occasion when some tentative followers were thinking of joining his ranks. "For which of you, intending to build a tower, does not first sit down and estimate the cost, to see whether he has enough to complete it? . . . Or what king, going out to wage war against another king, will not sit down first and consider whether he is able with ten thousand to oppose the one who comes against him with twenty thousand?" (Luke 14:28, 31).

I repeat, this is good sense, and on the whole I support it. Yet there's something in me that goes off like Don Quixote in *Man of La Mancha*, tilting at windmills and dreaming impossible dreams and throwing my energy into apparently hopeless causes. I should know better because I'm an Iowa boy, and in Iowa you're taught to deal with realities like harsh winters and scorching summers. Beyond that, I grew up in the Great Depression—but somehow in the midst of dreamers. My closest friend, Chris, was the son of Greek immigrants, parents whose English vocabulary couldn't have exceeded two or three hundred words. Yet he dreamed of being a radio announcer and a radio writer, two jobs that in those days required mastery of the English language and impeccable pronunciation. And my partner on the high school debate team, Sheldon Singer, was from a home almost as poor as mine and had as little prospect of going to college. But I still remember his prizewinning oration. "They tell us the frontiers are gone," it began; "that when the faint echoes of the last prairie schooner died out on the Dakota frontiers . . . ,"—and then Sheldon told us that the frontiers are *not* gone, and that we should all set out to build our castles in Spain. Count me a hopeless romantic, but as I recite those words to myself these many decades later, I want to find some new fields to conquer, some new cause in which I can enlist.

I'm sure that's one of the reasons I'm drawn to the Old Testament prophet Amos. Amos, like any foolish visionary, doesn't tell us any more about himself than is absolutely necessary, and what little he tells slips in almost by chance. I think he knows even as he thunders out his prophecies that he isn't likely to be heard, but he intends to speak his convictions, no matter.

It is when he is confronted by a member of the religious establishment that Amos gives us his own limited pedigree. "I am no prophet, nor a prophet's son, but I am a herdsman, and a dresser of sycamore trees" (Amos 7:14). Howard Moss, the longtime poetry editor of the *New Yorker* magazine, called Amos "the prototype of the populist who springs out of nowhere to condemn a civilization."[1] I like Moss's word, because I picture the populist as a product of the prairies. I know there have been urban populists, but for me the two words seem contradictory. I want my populist, my person of the people, to be close to the soil.

I must hasten to say that while I am a product of Iowa, I never lived on a farm. But I've come to have particular respect for farm people. I believe one has more time to think deeply when one has more solitude and when one is closer to the soil. When I read that the world is becoming more and more urban, I worry about it. It's not only that we lose something of our humanity if we live too close to too many people too much of the time; worse, I think we find it more difficult to know ourselves. We need to be alone now and then to remember our roots, or indeed to know our names. Then, knowing ourselves more intimately, we see the rest of the human race more clearly. We're able then to see people both more sympathetically and more realistically. We're more ready to weep for other people, but it's a tough weeping, the kind that knows we are at once pathetic, noble, and stupid.

So I see Amos as a man of the people, with a heart for their pain but with a painfully steady gaze in his evaluations. When he says that he was a herdsman and a dresser of sycamore trees, I recognize that he was not a property owner, or, if he was, his holdings were too small to really support him. One could be a herdsman the year round, while the dressing of sycamore trees was a seasonal matter and a short one at that. Maybe he did the tree dressing for supplemental income, or perhaps he was good enough at this work to make it worth his while to leave the herds for a period each year.

But somewhere along the way there had come to be a fire in his belly. Did it come to him full-force in one holy passion, unbidden, perhaps even resisted? Or was it a product of long observation, and hundreds of evenings of talking and listening with men like himself? I mean no sexual discrimination when I speak simply of "men"—I'm only acknowledging that in his world women and men didn't often mix in their visiting, so whatever talking he did was likely to be with other men.

When he speaks bitterly of "those who lie on beds of ivory, / and lounge on their couches" (Amos 6:4), I ask myself if he has observed this self-indulgent lifestyle for himself, or has he picked it up in the marketplace from passing travelers? Perhaps he had worked for the rich as a day laborer. In any case, it's clear that he's a man who's been taught to economize, so he feels contempt for those who "eat lambs from the flock, / and calves from the stall" (Amos 6:4); he wants us to know that if they had any sense they would wait until these creatures were full grown before butchering them. I used the word "contempt" a moment ago; Amos speaks with this mood again and again in his descriptions of the indifferent luxury of the people. Again, he reflects the agrarian mood; those of us who live in the cities or too near them are slowly inured to thoughtless waste—waste of resources, waste of time, waste of soul. Not Amos. For him such waste is not basically a matter of economics, but a matter of morality, and thus ultimately an issue to be dealt with before almighty God.

And the issue before God, as Amos saw it, was a human issue. What bothered him most was that all of this prodigal living was going on while the people were "not grieved over the ruin of Joseph" (Amos 6:6). I think Amos has two things in mind in his reference to Joseph. Immediately, he is using the term as a symbol of the whole people of

Israel. But I think he's also using "Joseph" the way a poet would, to remind us of the story of the young man who was sold into slavery by his brothers, who then sat down to finish their meal, contemplating the little pile of silver they had gained by their crime. In their small flush of luxury they felt no grief for Joseph.

But in all of this, Amos is tilting at windmills. The odds are all against his accomplishing anything. For one thing, he's a foreigner. He comes from Judah, the sister nation to Israel; and as any practical person knows, very few people welcome an outsider telling them about their shortcomings. It's true enough, of course, that a prophet is not without honor except in his own country, but it's also true that while most of us don't want to hear how bad we are, we especially don't want someone from the next county, state, or country doing it. Amaziah, a religious leader in Israel, put the matter clearly: "O seer, go, flee away to the land of Judah [that is, go back where you came from], earn your bread there, and prophesy there; but never again prophesy at Bethel, for it is the king's sanctuary, and it is a temple of the kingdom" (Amos 7:12–13).

And of course his message itself was unappealing. When people are prosperous, they don't want some irregular character telling them how they should spend their money. If there's any single subject about which people don't want to be reproved, it's their use of money. I suspect this may go back to some point in our teens when we're first feeling our sense of ownership, and our parents or some other older persons begin recommending economies to us. We're slow to get over that teenage reaction, "It's my money and I can do what I want with it." Those well-to-do Israelites liked veal and lamb and they didn't want someone telling them to eat beef and mutton. They loved showing neighbors their furniture with its embedded ivory. So Amos is a registered killjoy. No wonder Amaziah told him to go back home.

To the best of my knowledge, there's no evidence that Amos ever won the day with his call to social justice and economic restraint. So why do I think he's so admirable? Quite simply, because he was *right*, and what he said needed to be heard. I believe there are times when we don't need to win the battle, but we do need to speak the truth. If by chance we convince someone, God be praised; but if not, the truth as we see it has been spoken.

I cast my vote with Bonaro Overstreet. During the mid-twentieth century, she and her husband, Harry, wrote some best-selling advice on effective living, and somewhere along the way Mrs. Overstreet summed up her own philosophy of life this way:

> You say the little efforts that I make
> will do no good: they never will prevail
> to tip the hovering scale
> where Justice hangs in balance.
>   I don't think
> I ever thought they would.
> But I am prejudiced beyond debate
> in favor of my right to choose which side
> shall feel the stubborn ounces of my weight.[2]

Me too! I think my opinion is worth something. How much? Well, I suppose it depends on the degree of influence I have in a particular time or instance. But this much I know: the influence is *mine,* and I intend to decide where it will go. And because it is mine, it is eternally important to me. It's the only influence I am able to spend. It's possible, of course, that I can influence someone else in the use of that person's influence, but mine is the only weight I can claim as my own and use as my conscience directs me.

I want my influence to be registered for the matters in which I believe, the matters that seem to me to be important. I have to do this if I am to fulfill my human potential, to be my own person. I don't have to win, but I do have to feel that I've cast my lot on the side of my beliefs. I'd rather lose for the right than win for the wrong or to be in a majority with the indifferent.

There are so many matters in our present world where my contribution will make little difference, if any, yet where I feel I must do what is right, regardless. At repeated intervals we're told that there's an energy crisis. There will be, of course, until we find some way to replace the natural resources we are steadily moving toward exhaustion. I don't know what difference it makes if I turn out a light bulb, put down the thermostat a degree or two, turn off the faucet while I'm shaving, or use a little less gasoline. The cynic tells me that my quarter's worth won't solve the energy crisis, and of course the cynic is right, as cynics often are. And yet the world's resources are being used up by millions of people in just such "quarter's worth" segments.

The cynic will then remind me that "the other guy" isn't going to do anything to save, so why should I bother? For me, that's just the point. I don't intend to let "the other guy" get the stubborn ounces of my weight (that's why Overstreet called them *stubborn*). What the other person does or fails to do can neither justify nor condemn me. I must deal with my own sense of right and wrong, and I must keep that sense very sensitive. The energy crisis may not be solved by the gasoline I don't use; the church budget may not be accomplished by my personal pledge; the dirty city sidewalk may not be made clean simply because I carry my scrap paper or cleansing tissue to the corner trash can. But I intend to put the stubborn ounces of my weight on the side in which I believe. For the sake of my own self-respect, for the value in which I hold my opinion, I will put my weight behind my convictions.

And when I do, I can remind myself that the little I have done is more than would have been done if I hadn't done that much! A high school basketball team came into the locker room stinging from a 55 to 22 defeat. One player moaned, "I only made one basket." His coach wisely answered, "But if you hadn't, the score would have been 55 to 20." What we do may not be much. It may not win the game. But it is a weight—however small!—on the positive side. And however small my weight, I want it to be for the team, the cause, the Christ in whom I believe.

And while I confess myself only a stubborn idealist committed too often to lost causes, I have also to confess that I'm not altogether as naive as I pretend to be. You see, very few of humanity's great causes have been won by massive popular support. It seems that way, but in truth the crowd enthusiasm comes after the fact. The majority of humanity is almost always somewhere in the lethargic middle. The weight that tips the scales for good—or for evil!—comes from minorities at either end of the spectrum; the minorities who choose to make their weight felt. When good causes are lost, it is usually because good people haven't put their stubborn ounces to work, or have let their stubbornness lapse too soon.

I believe deeply in democracy. But I know well enough that the masses of people don't come up with ideas—they respond to ideas. The great body of people are not leaders, they are people waiting for leadership. That's why the weight of our stubborn ounces can some-day be crucially important. It may be that some conviction that impels us is an idea whose time has come, because at that moment the same germ of conviction may be lying dormant in the hearts of hundreds, perhaps thousands, of others. But someone has to verbalize the idea. It is just conceivable that the stubborn ounces of your weight or mine may start a very landslide for goodness. Almost everything of worth in our world has begun with the vision and conviction of one or two or a dozen people. No one can estimate what an ultimate weight may come from the pathetically feeble pressure of our stubborn ounces.

As for Amos, I can't tell you that he won the battle. But this I know. We're still quoting Amos today. Not just preachers and Sunday school teachers (a stalwart lot that shouldn't be downgraded by a word like "just"), but a whole continuing breed of idealists. They keep coming back to Amos, twenty-seven centuries later, because his courageous words give them heart and hope. One way or another, however, in his time Amos was going to declare his inextinguishable conviction. I think Amos, like Bonaro Overstreet, was "prejudiced beyond debate / in favor of [his] right to choose which side / should feel the stubborn ounces of [his] weight."

Me, too.

Chapter 8

Faithful for the Long Pull

Scripture Reading: Daniel 6:1–10

*T*hose of us who love music get a fringe benefit that is sometimes greater than the enjoyment of the music itself. I'm thinking of the memories that so easily wrap themselves around a fragment of a composition, whether the melody, the lyrics, or both. For some the connection is to an old school song, for another the song that was sung at his or her wedding or that an orchestra was playing when he or she fell in love. Some of us tear up when we remember a song our mother or father sang in our presence a long generation ago. I know of several movies I've forgotten, but whose theme music brings memories any time a rendition comes up on my car radio.

I have literally hundreds of such songs, sacred and secular, classical and common, honorable and ridiculous. And because the church and my faith have been such constant factors in my life, many of these musical memories are hymns. Some I seem to have known forever, but in other instances I can recall a particular time and place where the hymn blessed me in some ineffaceable way. That's the way it is with an old hymn by Phillip Bliss, one of the most popular hymnists of the nineteenth century. Nowadays when I sing this song, it's mostly to myself, in my automobile, because not many churches use it in this hurried twenty-first century. But that doesn't diminish my enjoyment. Somewhere in the first few words I transport myself back to June mornings in Iowa when I was perhaps eleven years old. Even at this moment I can feel the texture of the morning air on those first days of summer heat; the smell of our city streets asserts itself out of nowhere.

Specifically, my memory carries me to a little downtown Methodist church called "The Helping Hand Mission." If you had seen it you would wonder why I cherish the memory. The sanctuary (I doubt we ever called it that) was painfully simple, with no stained-glass windows and whose walls were adorned only by a biblical picture or two and a board reporting Sunday school statistics for the previous and current weeks. But each time I return to my hometown I make my way to 920 Fourth Street. A movie metroplex now stands where our little church used to be, but after I've stood there for a moment I can hear the song as we sang it those June mornings, at the conclusion of each session of our daily vacation Bible school:

> Dare to be a Daniel,
> > Dare to stand alone!
> Dare to have a purpose firm!
> Dare to make it known![1]

I knew all about Daniel. As the Bible tells the story, when Daniel was only a boy, probably an early teenager, his country was invaded by armies from Babylon, the dominant political and military power of the period. Daniel was carried captive to a strange land. The Babylonians were wise enough to see that some of the young Jewish men had notable potential, so they selected a few of them for special training for government service, along with selected Babylonian youths.

Before long the Jewish youths—there were four of them—faced a showdown. According to their faith, it was wrong to eat and drink certain foods and beverages, so they asked to be excused from the privileges of the scholars' training table. They were respectful in their appeal, but firm, so firm that their supervisor was persuaded to accept their petition. And they won! Although the diet they had chosen was exceedingly restricted, they were "better and fatter" than all the others (Dan. 1:15).

It was a great victory, but as it turned out it was only the first of Daniel's tests. The kings of Babylon, and later a king of Persia, trusted Daniel in quite extraordinary ways, but time and again he had to stand in the face of determined opposition. The climaxing incident, and the one for which Daniel is most remembered—especially in Sunday school stories!—came many years later. Once again Daniel was a leading figure in the government. The king had, in fact, selected three presidents to oversee the kingdom, and he was one of them. In time he became the leader and the most trusted in the group.

The most trusted, that is, by the king. Others in the presidium, and the one hundred twenty satraps below them, began to ask why a foreigner should be the king's favorite. They set in operation a plan to be rid of Daniel. In doing so, they paid him the highest possible compliment; it's ironical they didn't recognize it as such. "We shall not find any ground for complaint against this Daniel," they agreed among themselves, "unless we find it in connection with the law of his God" (Dan. 6:5). They knew that the only way they could discredit Daniel was by putting him in a position where loyalty to his faith would force him to be disloyal to the government.

So Daniel's enemies presented a plan to the king. They had been in the political process long enough to know how to do their business. They crafted their plan to appeal to the king's pride and vanity. These are vulnerable areas in most of us humans, and sometimes they are especially vulnerable areas in people who are accustomed to power. Power and adulation are to some people what money is to others— they can never get enough of them. So these clever men recommended to the king that for a period of thirty days no one was to petition any god or king except King Darius. If anyone violated this rule, he or she would be thrown into a den of lions. King Darius saw nothing wrong in the proposal; he saw only that these people were trying to gain for him the credit he knew he so rightly deserved. So he signed the document into law.

So what did Daniel do when the law was announced? Well, what would you do if your faith became a life-and-death issue? I'll tell you what Daniel did, in case you've forgotten the story. He did just what he had always done. The Hebrew Scriptures put it perfectly: "Although Daniel knew that the document had been signed, he continued to go to his house, which had windows in its upper room open toward Jerusalem, and to get down on his knees three times a day to pray to his God and praise him, just as he had done previously" (Dan. 6:10). Daniel's enemies were watching, of course, so they apprehended him almost immediately. The king cared deeply for Daniel. He wanted to release him, but the laws of the land had to be maintained, for so it was with the laws of the Medes and the Persians.

So they threw Daniel into the lions' den and sealed the entrance with the king's signet ring. The Bible says that the king spent a miserable, sleepless night, sad that he was losing his friend and confidant and most able public servant, Daniel, and probably ashamed of his own part in the matter. Who knows, perhaps he was sorry even for the vanity that had gotten him into such a mess—though I'm asking a lot of Darius to come to such a realization, because vanity is a sin that even saints find it hard to recognize and even harder to acknowledge.

Early the next morning, at the very dawning of the day, the king hurried to what he thought had been the place of execution. When he looked into the den, however, he found that Daniel was safe in the midst of the hungry creatures.

> Dare to be a Daniel,
>> Dare to stand alone!
> Dare to have a purpose firm!
> Dare to make it known!

I remember the vigor and certainty with which I sang those words as a preteen-ager. And yes, the naïveté. I had no idea how difficult it would be to "be a Daniel." I didn't know how often my best resolves would be tested, or how confusing it would sometimes be to determine the ground where my firm stands should be taken. I only knew that I wanted to be a Daniel, to stand for God even if it meant standing alone. And, of course, I had no emotional basis for grasping how "alone" might feel. "Alone" sings better than it feels.

But as naive as that boy was so long ago, he was on the right track. I'm sorry that Phillip Bliss's hymn is so seldom sung these days. Yes, I know it is simple in both text and tune, but certainly no simpler than a good deal else that is being sung; and I'm very sure the Daniel-mood is needed. When the late Peter Marshall was chaplain of the United States Senate, he once prayed, "Lord, help us to stand for something lest we fall for anything." God knows we're inclined these days to fall for almost anything, especially if it's advertised or publicized long enough and enticingly enough—and no doubt this is partly because we stand for so little.

Mind you, we do stand up for some things. Some of us are outspoken in defense of our favorite baseball, football, or basketball team, and some of us only a little less vehemently about an automobile brand or a golf club. But so often we grow silent if a moral issue is raised or a human being is unjustly defamed. Under such circumstances we find it easy to retreat into silence.

Several factors complicate this mood in our time. For one, a particular kind of broad-mindedness is a major virtue in our culture. I agree readily that I prefer a broad-minded person to a narrow-minded one. But above all, I want persons to demonstrate that they have a mind, and that they have bothered to give their mind enough to work on that they have a right to an opinion, so that their breadth is not embarrassingly shallow. We need to know how to listen intently and deeply to the other person's point of view, and to be ready to change our minds when another opinion is demonstrably better. But we ought never to be so open-minded that we are without convictions, especially on issues that really, deeply, eternally matter.

Another philosophy of our times is the happy idea that everyone has a right to his or her opinion. This is, of course, true but it doesn't mean that every opinion is of the same worth. My opinions on technical matters are of no consequence; it's better that I keep these opinions to myself. It's also quite possible that the person with remarkable technical intelligence is not a specialist in ethical judgments. It is important to respect everyone's right to an opinion without a sentimentality that says each opinion is to be equally prized. When it comes to those matters that have to do with one's own soul, one ought to be ready to take a position. Graciously, but nonetheless with certainty.

Where did Daniel get the inner strength to have convictions about right and wrong? Some might calculate that he was simply a cantankerous person, generally spoiling for a fight. Not so. When we read his story and see how he responded to those who differed with him, we're impressed that he was a particularly gracious man, with a gentility that is rather rare in our time. Deep convictions don't require poor manners to express. To the contrary, the person who is at peace with his or her convictions may find it easier to stand by them graciously. So what was Daniel's secret? How is it that he became a person held up for admiration?

As a starter, consider this: Daniel's character formation began when he was young. If we hope someday to deal victoriously with life's major tests, we do well to enter training as early as possible. If we're late, we can do some things to make up for lost time, but there's a great deal to be said for an early start. And with his early start, Daniel formed good habits. He gladly imposed strict dietary regulations on himself as a very young man. Clearly, he did the same with his spiritual habits. Consider again the tribute Daniel's enemies paid him: they knew him by his good habits. They knew he was so faithful in his prayers that they could be sure of the time of day when he would pray. What they didn't know was that Daniel's prayers gave him the strength to carry him through any crisis his enemies might inflict on him. They had no idea how powerful right habits can be.

And with his early start and his good habits, Daniel was tough. In another time we were often reminded that Karl Marx described religion as an opiate for the masses. In truth, biblical religion is just the opposite. It gives people a clear-eyed view of life with all its hazards, including a good many dangers other people rarely see. Then it gives them the courage to meet those hazards and to be victorious in the midst of them. Biblical faith helps us to live dangerously. Ask Dietrich Bonhoeffer, or Desmond Tutu. Ask those thousands of persons who dare to meet in house churches that have not gotten government approval. They wouldn't boast about it, but they offer dramatic evidence that good faith makes one tough, right at the core of one's being.

Daniel was made tough by what the Sunday school song described as "a purpose firm." A human being is very rich when he or she has a worthy purpose in life. Daniel had such a purpose. He was dedicated to God and to fulfilling God's will in his life. Someone has said, "I would rather die young for a worthy cause than to live long for nothing." Daniel would understand that. As a result, he had a moral compass that headed him Godward, no matter where the tide of the times might pull.

But I haven't yet said what impresses me most about Daniel. He was faithful for the long haul. In that boyhood church of mine, as perhaps in yours, there was a popular painting of Daniel in the lions' den. In that painting, Daniel was a young man, perhaps just out of his teens. But as the Bible tells the story, by the time of the lions' den Daniel was well into his Social Security years. We don't know what happened to the three friends who began the journey with Daniel. We have no reason to think they dropped by the wayside, but it's likely enough they had died or had been given less auspicious positions. If so, I suspect Daniel might have wished, as he faced the challenge of his later years, that they were still with him.

But, you see, Daniel had outlasted kings and empires. When we first meet Daniel, Nebuchadnezzar of Babylon was king; then Belshazzar, and at last King Darius of Persia. Daniel's story began when he was a boy in his homeland, and continued through the days of his captivity first to the Babylonians and at last to the Medes and Persians. So when we come to the lions' den, Nebuchadnezzar is gone, Belshazzar is gone, and the Babylonian empire is history. But Daniel is still here. We can say the same thing about the church. Empires have come and gone in the past twenty centuries, but still there is the church. Daniel's life is a kind of microcosm of the whole empire of faith.

Faith is for the long haul, you know. The Christian life is not a hundred-yard dash; it is not even the Boston Marathon. If you want to give it a name, call it the New Jerusalem Marathon. We belong to a cause that extends from generation to generation through revivals and losses, through heresies and divisions, through prayer and through failure. Just as it is, too, in our individual lives.

I loved Daniel when I was a boy back in Iowa. He was my hero because I saw him as someone not much older than myself. And as a matter of fact, that's where his story begins in the Bible. But today, as a somewhat older man, I love Daniel more than ever. I understand him better now, at this point in my life, than I did as an eleven-year-old. Because I've come to appreciate the long haul of the Christian faith, I've come to admire those good and godly people who give their lives, over all their years, to being the best that, by the grace of God, they can be.

In the process, I've learned that if one is to be a Daniel, one must be ready not only for the rather glamorous lions' den, but for the everyday business of living. We don't know what Daniel did in the years between the several dramatic stories in the book that bears his name, but I offer an opinion: I believe Daniel stood as firm in the days of ordinary life as he did in the life-threatening crises. You may have noticed in reading the refrain from the Phillip Bliss hymn that it is a song marked by exclamation points. I honor that punctuation, but in truth the Christian life is lived mostly with commas and dashes and semicolons.

Because, you see, a good many of our lions are pussycats, but the peril remains. We have to live our faith in the daily routine of our job, our school, our marriage or singleness, our town, our dinner party, our stop at the coffeehouse. It doesn't sound terribly heroic, but most of the time we meet our lions in ordinary places, and only rarely do they look like lions. It is in such places, however, that the kingdom of God is won and lost. It is in such places that we have to "Dare to be a Daniel, dare to stand alone! Dare to have a purpose firm! Dare to make it known!"

Chapter 9

Living on Borrowed Time

Scripture Reading: Luke 2:25–35

Of course, we're all living on borrowed time. None of us has paid for the years we're privileged to live on this planet, nor are we given any guarantee as to how long our tenures will be. The actuarial tables give us some odds for calculating, but we know they're no better than predicted scores before a football game. We would be presumptuous if we suggested (as some do sometimes) that we deserve more, because most of us are smart enough to know that all of life is a gift. In that sense, it's all borrowed time.

But now and then some person comes to the very face of death and, quite miraculously, the event is postponed. Sometimes such a person concludes his or her life has been spared for a purpose. Some feel it so strongly that they go into a service occupation, hoping they can pay the debt. Others continue the usual course of life, but with a sense of life's sacredness that most people never feel. I think of a man who lived through a teenage accident where his closest friend was killed; he said ever after that he felt he had to "live for two."

I want to tell you about a man who felt he was living on borrowed time and who acknowledged the debt with gladness, so that when his postponed exit came he was so satisfied and so fulfilled that he welcomed the prospect of death. He knew his purpose on earth was complete, and knowing as much, he gladly turned in his time card. I don't know if he had gone through some climactic, near-death experience; the Bible doesn't give us any such detail. We have no sure data to help us understand why he felt as he did about his life. We only know that God promised him he wouldn't die until he got what he wanted.

Prior to that reference, we don't really know much about him. He gets no introduction beyond the place in which he lived. Listen: "Now there was a man in Jerusalem whose name was Simeon" (Luke 2:25). We know nothing of his ancestry, his social standing, or his work. The Bible frequently tells us the tribe from which a person comes; in fact, it does so with the woman who shares the scene with Simeon in Luke's report. Anna, we're told, was "the daughter of Phanuel, of the tribe of Asher" (Luke 2:36). We're also told that Anna was a woman "of a great age," and that she had been a widow since seven years after her marriage, and had now reached the age of eighty-four (vv. 36–37), but we're given no such data about Simeon. People seem to assume he was an older man. Artists always depict him with a flowing white beard. T. S. Eliot described him as "one who had eighty years and no tomorrow."[1]

But the Bible doesn't say so. I suspect we draw our conclusions because of the promise he had received, "that he would not see death before he had seen the Lord's Messiah" (Luke 2:26). We naturally conclude that this means he was an older person. But that isn't necessarily so. In truth, he could have been a middle-aged person whose health was so perilous that he felt death was imminent. Indeed, he might even have been quite young, yet suffering under such a death threat. I won't press the matter, largely because—probably like you—I enjoy this picture of the serene old man. In truth, come to think about it, I've preached sermons and even included a chapter in a book where I so imagined him. But actually, we don't really know how old Simeon was.

However, since I am myself getting older, I will venture a prejudice of age. The Bible also says that he was "righteous and devout" (Luke 2:25), and that's more likely as one grows older. Mind you, I'm not saying this on the basis of any movement of my own toward godliness; God forbid! I'm thinking, rather, of people I've known over the years of my life. There are very few sudden saints; godliness is a fruit that matures slowly. On that ground, I'll accept that Simeon was very possibly an older man. Perhaps even—like Anna—very old.

And I am for sure impressed that the Bible describes him as being "righteous and devout." This tells so very much about the kind of human being he was. It describes him, not by his striking appearance, nor by his community standing or the first-century equivalent of his stock portfolio, but by something intangible and terribly hard to define. "Righteous" isn't a popular word in our day. Has it occurred to you that when we use the word it is most often with the preface "self," as in "self-righteous"? I don't think that's because there are more self-righteous people than there used to be; I think it's simply that righteousness itself is not one of the hot commodities in the public square—hence the major use of the word is in its negative application.

That's strange, because in a sense "righteous" is not an exclusively religious word. To be righteous, in the truest biblical sense, is to be *right*, not in the way one claims to be right in the course of a discussion, but right in the way a computer or an engine is right when it runs properly. Or, more to the point, the way a *life* operates when it is running properly. Somehow we get the idea that qualities like righteousness are nice supplementary features for a life, when in truth they are essential equipment. We realize as much when we get close to a person who is clearly righteous; we see a kind of holy efficiency in such a life that makes the whole structure run better.

And if "righteous" is a hard word for us to apply to life's daily run, I suspect that "devout" is still more off-putting. But to be devout means nothing other, of course, than to be *devoted* to something. Most of us acknowledge that life is at its best when we have found something that captures our deepest devotion, and what better, surely, than the ultimate—God? So we generally associate the word "devout" with matters of deep piety, and rightly so. Someone who is devout is someone whose religious life is not something superficial, worn for public occasions or to impress others, but something that characterizes the very person. Think for a moment: how many persons have you known for whom you would choose the adjective "devout" as the word best describing them? "Nice" people, "good" people, "honorable," "upright," "kind"—all admirable terms, mind you, that I would be glad to have attached to me. But they lack the quality of holy gravitas that is conveyed by "devout."

These are the words the Gospel of Luke uses to describe Simeon. Perhaps what ought to impress us most is that we use these words so rarely to describe the people we know; and perhaps what ought to sadden us most is that this is so. Would that we knew more people to whom we could apply these adjectives! Still more, would that we were more committed to having others so define and describe us!

But perhaps the reason we aren't more impressed with words like "righteous" and "devout" is because we've been inclined to see them rather exclusively as inward words, that is, as words that describe goodness, true enough, but goodness that seems centered on its owner. Nothing could be farther from the truth if we are using these terms in a truly Christian sense. Simeon's quality was demonstrated in the fact that he was "looking forward to the consolation of Israel." Specifically, "[i]t had been revealed to him by the Holy Spirit that he would not see death before he had seen the Lord's Messiah" (Luke 2:26). Simeon was no isolated saint, seeking to accumulate personal holy favor; he was a man who loved his people so passionately that he wanted above all that they should enjoy God's "consolation" in the coming of the long-awaited Messiah.

Was this so extraordinary? It's hard to say, because of course it's hard to know how people were thinking twenty centuries ago. We do know, however, that the religious scholars of the time were alive to the issue. When the wise men came to Jerusalem looking for the new-born king of the Jews, the chief priests and scribes were quick to report that according to the prophet Micah the promised Messiah would be in the town of Bethlehem (Matthew 2:1–6). Were there many who pursued this knowledge? We don't know. We have no reliable way to estimate the number of persons who were awaiting the coming of the Messiah, or the degree of intensity with which they waited.

But there's no question about the manner of Simeon's waiting. Something about the intensity of his faith and the depth of his longing was unique, or nearly so. I suspect this is always the stuff that saints are made of. Francis Thompson, the late nineteenth-century English poet, knew something of the torments of the lost and the wonders of experiencing God, as indicated in his classic poem "The Hound of Heaven." He put the matter almost perfectly: "To most, even good people, God is a belief. To the saints he is an embrace." I have a feeling that Thompson's words describe Simeon. Here was a person who longed for God—and for the purposes of God in our world—in a fashion quite beyond the ordinary run. His belief was deep and profound, but it was also passionate beyond understanding.

And let me underline again the selfless quality of Simeon's seeking. He wanted to see the Messiah, but his desire was focused beyond himself. A person can be as selfish in seeking spiritual blessing as in the pursuit of stocks, bonds, and Riviera mansions. The Pharisees whom Jesus excoriated were men who sought God with a passion, but in some cases it was a very selfish passion. Not so Simeon. His hunger for the Messiah was not for his own benefit, but for his people. I have chosen my words here carefully. I could have said, "for his nation," because he was a true Israelite and it was Israel's Messiah that he sought. But as Luke describes Simeon, and as Simeon's song reveals his character, he wasn't seeking the conquering Messiah that many of his countrymen quite naturally hoped for, so I use the term "people" rather than the political term, "nation."

In fact, when at last Simeon put his dream into a song, he included in his embrace not only his own people, Israel, but the rest of the world. For the Jew, the world was made up of two parts, Jews and Gentiles. Simeon described the Messiah as "a light for revelation to the Gentiles / and for glory to your people Israel" (Luke 2:32). In his understanding of the Messiah's role, Simeon was well ahead of many of Jesus' first followers, who had to struggle to accept the Gentiles as part of God's eternal purpose.

Here and there in my life I have met people with the breadth of a Simeon. I'm not speaking now of the remarkable spiritual perception that characterized him, but rather this quality of acceptance that so easily united his beloved people with those who were so unlike his people. What gives a person such breadth and heart? We like to think that education is the secret, but it's only partly true. I have known some admirably literate people who spoke the proper language of acceptance but who kept an antiseptic distance from those who were different. On the other hand, I've known people who wouldn't know how to enunciate a philosophy of world brotherhood and sisterhood, but who, because their nature is so inclusive, see worth in all people. Simeon was such a person, and he believed the Messiah would introduce such a quality into our planet.

So Simeon waited for the Messiah, and waited with such pure, selfless desire that God revealed to him that "he would not see death before he had seen the Lord's Messiah." The Bible gives no hint as to how long Simeon had waited. Was it a year, a decade, a score of years? Did he sometimes watch a state parade and wonder if the person leading the procession might be the one? Or did his faith reach farther, so that sometimes, sharing in a coming-of-age celebration with a Jewish boy, he dreamed that this might someday be the one?

Then one day it happened. In the temple. In my judgment this was the likely place, but of course I'm prejudiced, because I've been a professional religious worker nearly all my life. But it's not a matter purely of prejudice; other things being equal, one should expect that the plan of God would consummate in the house of God. We don't know how Simeon happened to be in the temple on this particular day. Perhaps he always came; that's a good strategy for not missing something important—just be there! And God's whisper came in his ear: There's the one.

A baby. By all outward judgments, a quite ordinary baby. Judging, that is, by the parents—a rather typical teenage girl, first-time mother, and a tradesman who stood awkwardly beside her. They didn't seem marked for prominence. But this was it. The voice of God in Simeon's soul was utterly beyond argument. This was it. This was the Holy Family.

Luke reports that Simeon took the baby in his arms and began to praise God. I suspect Simeon's action wasn't quite so unnerving an action in the first-century Middle Eastern world as it would be in ours; older people had such standing in that culture that parents would not necessarily be shocked by, and certainly wouldn't resist, an elderly stranger entering their sacred rite. His words are familiar to many of us, especially in the rhythms of the King James Version of the Bible:

> Lord, now lettest thou thy servant depart in peace, according to thy word:
> For mine eyes have seen thy salvation,
> Which thou hast prepared before the face of all people;
> A light to lighten the Gentiles, and the glory of thy people Israel.
> (Luke 2:29–32, KJV)

But then Simeon went from the wonder of a promise fulfilled—a promise larger than either he or the wondering parents could grasp—

to a fearful word spoken specifically to Mary, concluding, "And a sword will pierce your own soul too" (Luke 2:35). I think most of us assume that this strange word was fulfilled for Mary at the crucifixion of her son. Mary had to feel the darkness in Simeon's final words, but perhaps only a poet could venture her feelings of incongruity at such a dissonant word on an otherwise perfect day.

If I dared, I would envy Simeon. God took him into the divine confidence, allowing him to know the times and the seasons in a fashion and degree not granted to the rest of us mortals. I suspect it is because this otherwise unknown man longed so earnestly for the purposes of God, and longed with such purity and unselfishness that he could be trusted. Lesser mortals would have exploited such an experience; in our day, it would put a person on a lecture circuit, or at least on the cover of a religious publication. As for Simeon, with the baby in his arms he was now ready to die. I doubt that he would have put it this way, but Simeon had been living to see God's will come to pass. He believed that with the Messiah's coming the purposes of God were assured. Now that this was settled, he was ready to die. He could go in peace.

Two thousand years later, Simeon's words—as Luke recorded them—are quoted daily in almost every part of the world. Within the Catholic Church his Nunc Dimittis is said every night in the compline, the closing part of the Divine Office. A variety of churches in other traditions sing the lines as part of the closing blessing at Sunday worship. How many people have spoken words so special that they are quoted every day, in thousands of places? These are the words of a person who thought at some time that he was about to die—perhaps because he was so old or so sick. But God loaned him extra time, because this single-minded man wanted to see God's will come to pass. And when he saw it, he was ready to die. If you have lived for the will of God, and you have seen it come to pass—indeed, have held it in your arms!—it is indeed time to exit right.

Chapter 10

Friend of the Bridegroom

Scripture Reading: John 1:6–9, 3:22–30

*I*f ever a person had "Success" written all over the Application for Admission to Life, it was the person we have come to know as John the Baptist. Mind you, the world in which he was promised success was a very small one, but I've come to realize that we all live in very small worlds. The latest person to win a platinum award in the recording world probably doesn't know the name of the Nobel Prize winner in economics; and, although it might surprise that platinum winner, the Nobel recipient probably doesn't know her name.

Still, in his particular small world, John had everything imaginable going for him. His mother and father were both descended from the family of Aaron, brother of Moses and founding member, so to speak, of the Jewish priesthood. In a nation where religious leadership was the one continuing reality and where at crucial times its influence exceeded that of any political leader, this was indeed the ultimate aristocracy.

More than that, however, John's parents were truly good people. Some people born into aristocratic lines have been embarrassed that theirs was not a moral aristocracy; not so with John. Of his parents it was said that they "were righteous before God, living blamelessly according to all the commandments and regulations of the Lord" (Luke 1:6).

I hate to pile on any further evidence, lest I seem to overdo, but there's one more thing, and from a faith point of view it's the biggest of all. John was a miracle baby. His parents were beyond childbearing age and had never been able to conceive when Zechariah, John's father, was told that he and Elizabeth were going to have a son. And what a son! "[M]any will rejoice at his birth, for he will be great in the sight of the Lord" (Luke 1:14–15). Even before his birth he would be filled with the Holy Spirit; and it was predicted before his conception that people would see in him "the spirit and power of Elijah"—which was to say, he would have the dynamism of Israel's most charismatic prophet, the one who was to have a special relationship to the ministry of the Messiah. When he was born, his father was so moved that he spoke ecstatically of God's purposes in this son, declaring that he would be "called the prophet of the Most High":

> "for you will go before the Lord to prepare his ways,
> to give knowledge of salvation to his people
> by the forgiveness of their sins." (Luke 1:76–77)

John grew up in what we would see as a hill country village, but in a highly literate and deeply spiritual home. I don't know how much his parents told him about the unique circumstances of his birth. I can't help thinking they would have shared some of the story with him, but at the very least they would have raised him in such a way that he would have sensed instinctively a kind of holy responsibility. There's evidence of this in the author's summary of his early years: "The child grew and became strong in spirit" (Luke 1:80). That's a key word, believe me. As the years and his work unfolded, he would need to be strong in spirit. Herculean, in fact.

That's as much as we really know about John's growing up, but in a sense it's all we need to know. Because for a person like John the story isn't really about where he went to school or the people he knew, but the development of his character. The Gospel of John (no relation) pays this John an intriguing compliment. When the writer introduces the Lord Christ, it is with language that is at once philosophy and poetry: "In the beginning was the Word, and the Word was with God, and the Word was God." But after proceeding in such sublime form for several sentences, he interrupts himself to say, "There was a man sent from God, whose name was John. He came as a witness to testify to the light, so that all might believe through him" (John 1:6–7). Then, just as abruptly, almost as if unconscious of the interruption, the writer continues talking about Christ.

What kind of person is this John, that the Gospel writer slips so easily from the magnificent language of eternity to the relatively mundane statement "There was a man sent from God, whose name was John"? As his public career begins, he is a wilderness preacher. Much of the time he lives in one of the most terrible deserts in the world, a place where the limestone rock shimmers in the heat and where it sounds almost hollow to the foot, as if there were some furnace beneath it.

To choose such a setting seems a request for failure. Instead of establishing headquarters in some central location where he could get the endorsement of authority figures, he appeared to isolate himself. When we read how several New Testament writers describe his appearance and diet, we might easily think John was intentionally eccentric. But somehow people heard of him and went to him. If anyone has demonstrated that if ever a person wrote a better book, preached a better sermon, or built a better mousetrap, the world would beat a path to his door even if he built his house in the woods, it was this John.

Nor did he do anything to cater to those who sought him out. As his title indicates, he baptized those who were ready to make a religious commitment. But it looks almost as if he wanted to drive people away, rather than to win them. "You brood of vipers!" he cried. "Who warned you to flee from the wrath to come? Bear fruits worthy of repentance." He knew that many of his listeners took great pride in their Jewish heritage. They got no comfort or endorsement from him. "Do not begin to say to yourselves [it was as if he were reading their minds], 'We have Abraham as our ancestor'; for I tell you, God is able from these stones to raise up children to Abraham" (Luke 3:7–8).

Eventually the religious power structure sent a delegation. There was common agreement that he was a prophet of God, but somehow even that exalted designation wasn't enough to explain this strange, sometimes frightening man. When they asked him, "Who are you?" the inference in their question was clear, and John answered with equal clarity: "I am not the Messiah." Was he then Elijah, or perhaps the prophet described by Moses? No. So in exasperation they returned to their original question: "Who are you?"

He had already said that he was "the voice of one crying out in the wilderness," preparing the way for the Lord; now he became more explicit. "I baptize with water. Among you stands one whom you do not know, the one who is coming after me; I am not worthy to untie the thong of his sandal" (John 1:26–27). It is as if a political convention were about to name their presidential candidate, only to have the person object, "I'm just here to introduce the candidate you're really looking for."

It happened the next day. John saw Jesus, the Nazareth carpenter, coming toward him, and declared, "Here is the Lamb of God who takes away the sin of the world!" After a few more words he concluded, "And I myself have seen and testified that this is the Son of God" (John 1:29, 34).

I don't know how the crowds responded to this. Perhaps they saw John's unwillingness to accept adulation as still more evidence of his eccentricity; after all, he seemed to be set on offending more often than on building a following. Besides, when a candidate not only says, "I do not choose to run," but even endorses an alternative—and an unknown one at that—it's probably time to begin looking elsewhere.

It looks as if that was the conclusion reached not only by the casual crowd, but even some who had seemed most drawn to the wilderness preacher. The day following, when John again identified Jesus as "the Lamb of God," two of his disciples followed Jesus, to seek conversation with him. It was the beginning of Jesus' inner circle, the Twelve. Faithful followers are hard to come by; some of John's best were now leaving.

Before long Jesus began baptizing people. This is the only place in the New Testament story that speaks of Jesus baptizing; it seems almost as if he were setting out to compete with John, because baptism was John's distinguishing act, the apparent focus of his preaching. Some of John's loyal followers reported what they had heard. "Rabbi, the one who was with you across the Jordan, to whom you testified, here he is baptizing, and all are going to him" (John 3:26). The messengers were engaging in the hyperbole of disaster, the kind of language people use when they're upset and just a bit irrational. "All" were not going to Jesus; the writer has just told us that "people kept coming" to John, "and were being baptized" (John 3:22). But for the men who loved John and believed in him—and who of course had their own stake in his ministry—for them, the apparently competing ministry from the Nazareth carpenter was very upsetting.

It is at this point that John's deeply embedded strength showed itself. "No one can receive anything except what has been given from heaven," he said. "You yourselves are my witnesses that I said, 'I am not the Messiah, but I have been sent ahead of him.' He who has the bride is the bridegroom. The friend of the bridegroom, who stands and hears him, rejoices greatly at the bridegroom's voice. For this reason my joy has been fulfilled. He must increase, but I must decrease" (John 3:27–30).

I can't imagine a more powerful statement of discipleship or of loyalty. It's interesting that John said earlier, before Jesus had been identified, that he wasn't worthy "to untie the thong of his sandal" (John 1:27). The figure of speech John used on that occasion makes one think of Jesus' act at the Last Supper when he washed the feet of his disciples. When John could have insisted on position and prominence, he chose, figuratively speaking, to fall at Jesus' feet.

The picture evoked by John's language was more vivid for his disciples than for us. In their world, the friend of the bridegroom served as liaison between bride and bridegroom and took care of details great and small, all the way from delivering invitations and arranging the wedding to presiding at the wedding feast. But especially, he guarded the bridal chamber to prevent any intruder from entering until, recognizing in the darkness the bridegroom's voice, he let him in. Then his job was done. This was the way John saw his divine calling.

If I could, I would now exit from the story. From the point of view of either a devout Christian or a warmly sentimental soul, John's story is nicely packaged at this point. He doesn't have the kind of acclaim his birth credentials seemed to promise, but he has had his glory days when the crowds formed a steady, if erratic, road to the wilderness to see him. Now that his hour of glory is past, he has demonstrated sterling character in stepping aside to make room for Jesus of Nazareth. But life isn't often as tidy as a simple melodrama, so we can't drop the curtain just yet.

John was not an eccentric, as I have dared to hint along the way; he was simply a fearless preacher, who used all his unique gifts to declare the truth as he saw it. He wouldn't step down for anyone—including Herod, whose kingdom was small, but one where he had nearly absolute power. So when John condemned Herod publicly for marrying his sister-in-law, wife to his brother Philip, Herod threw him in prison.

I think John must have known that his kind of preaching would someday get him in serious trouble. People in high places grow so accustomed to adulation that they become hypersensitive to criticism, to a point where they find it hard to understand that anyone could think badly of them. But John had always preached the truth as he saw it, and he didn't seem to worry who was in his congregation. Nevertheless, persecution anticipated and persecution experienced are two quite different matters. In prison he had plenty of time to evaluate his life and work. Among the dark and creepy, crawly things that inhabit a prison cell, nothing is worse than self-doubt. John began to doubt.

Worst of all, he began to doubt the very purpose of his life. From as far back, I venture, as he could remember, John had known what he was to do: not simply to be a wilderness prophet, or to baptize the repentant, or even to challenge sin in high places. Above all, he was to prepare the way for the Messiah. He had done so, and he had done it with magnificent abandon. When his most devoted followers told him his popularity ratings were going down, John said in effect, "This is just what I had expected and hoped for. I'm the friend of the bridegroom, and now that the bridegroom is here, I will begin making my exit."

But in prison the words no longer sounded so devil-may-care. John began to analyze what Jesus was doing, the reports of which were coming to him third- and fourth-hand. The crowds were growing, they said; the teaching was exciting. But an aching pain was growing in John's heart, the pain many have felt when the end is near and they're wondering if the candle has been worth the burning. So John sent a message to Jesus via some of his disciples: "Are you the one who is to come, or are we to wait for another?" (Matt. 11:3).

This doesn't sound like the man who could live in an untamed wilderness on a diet of locusts and wild honey. His words lack the challenging audacity of "You vipers, why have you come to hear me preach?" Is this the same man who said, "Behold the Lamb of God!

He must increase, but I must decrease"? The same; have no doubt about it. You must have great capacity for doubt and terror if you would have great capacity for faith and sacrifice.

Jesus sent back a message of gracious reassurance. As the messengers left, Jesus told the assembled crowds how he felt about John. He would answer a question that had been in the minds and conversations of the people since John first came into prominence: Yes, "he is Elijah who is to come" (Matt. 11:14). But before that: "Truly I tell you, among those born of women no one has arisen greater than John the Baptist." Then Jesus added a word that signaled the end of one age and the beginning of another: "yet the least in the kingdom of heaven is greater than he" (Matt. 11:11).

Which is to say, John was right. He was the friend of the bridegroom. Now that the bridegroom had come, a new era had begun. And with it, Christ would increase and John would decrease.

Still, the more I think about John, the bigger he gets. The more he chooses to decrease, the larger he looms on my screen. You can't get much bigger than to realize the boundaries of your calling and to be content when those boundaries suddenly seem to crowd you almost out of existence. John was big enough to know who he was, and to love it. He was the friend of the Bridegroom, and he wanted nothing more.

Chapter 11

The Soldier–Theologian

Scripture Reading: Matthew 8:5–13 (Luke 7:1–10)

We preachers like to say that every Christian is a theologian. Of course, this is quite a countercultural position. Ours is an era of specialization in which, to adapt an old phrase, most of us come to know more and more about less and less until at last we know practically everything about next to nothing. The play-by-play announcers for a football game remind us that the players have to learn literally scores of intricate plays. The lineman who once needed only to get in the way of the person opposite him must now handle that process with all the nuances of a ballet artist. We know this is so because we see the quarterback looking at notes on his wristband with the same intensity as the secretary of state studying her script at an international press conference. It is, I repeat, a wonderfully and frighteningly specialized world in which you and I now live.

So how do I dare to suggest that every Christian is a theologian? In a culture where professional theologians possess a doctor of philosophy degree and often spend years pursuing apparently minute issues, how can every pew holder claim theological standing? If I were cynical, I'd say that this is just one of the catchphrases of our time. But in truth, this idea wasn't invented in a denominational public relations office. Protestants see it as part of Martin Luther's concept of the priesthood of all believers. Students of church history remember periods in the fourth and fifth centuries when bakers and shoemakers talked theology the way men now discuss the pennant race. And, come to think of it, the grand theological questions that challenge us come mostly from letters the apostle Paul once wrote to average believers—men and women and children, slaves and farmers and shopkeepers—in the first-century world. Obviously the apostle thought his believers in Corinth or Ephesus or Thessalonica could talk theology, so why can't we? Whether the times are specialized or not doesn't really matter; theology is the stuff of daily life, stuff as fundamental as our purpose in living and our reason for getting up in the morning. And along with that, it tells us how we deal with life and death and human tragedy.

Which brings us to my hero of the moment, a great soldier-theologian.

I'm sorry I can't tell you his name. The Bible doesn't bother to do so, so I won't try to fill the gap. Two Gospel writers, Matthew and Luke, tell the story, and both of them refer to this man simply as a centurion. This should probably make us feel right at home with the story, because we're often told that contemporary casual conversations—at a bridge party, a ball game, a convention, or with an airplane seat partner—move within minutes to the question, "What do you do for a living?" This man did military for a living. He was a centurion.

Let me tell you about centurions. Your dictionary will say that the term comes from the ancient Roman army, a commander of a century—that is, a hundred men. That's the fact, but it's about like saying an eagle is a bird. In practice, it could rightly be said that the centurion *was* the Roman army. The effectiveness and character of the centurions determined the success of the Roman army; and because of the way Rome ruled, the centurions determined ultimately the success of the Roman Empire. They were what we would call career soldiers. The discipline of the regiments depended on them. I suspect that many of the men who made up the Roman army were no better than they had to be. A large number were probably serving unwillingly. At any given moment they could be susceptible to trouble. In my years as a pastor I became increasingly convinced of the wisdom of the Creator in giving our human race both women and men. Let a group be made up of only one sex or the other, and before long particular undesirable traits appear. In the case of an entirely male group, a certain crudeness easily surfaces; the veneer of civilization seems very thin. Anyone who could take one hundred men, who are far from home and whose circumstances are often perilous, with life cheap, and can shape them into an effective, productive body deserves great admiration.

The late William Barclay pointed out what is for me a particularly significant fact, that every centurion mentioned in the New Testament is portrayed in an act of honor. He reminds us, for example, of the centurion at the crucifixion who recognized Jesus as the Son of God, and of the centurion who rescued Paul from a mob that was about to make an end of him, and the centurion who accompanied Paul with such courtesy on his journey to Rome.

But it's this soldier-theologian who fascinates me. I like him because he could look at the ordinary composition of his daily life and see in it truths of God and eternity. I admit a prejudice for this kind of person. I'm not thinking exclusively about religious matters. I like a person who, when discussing a player's hitting streak, has a comment beyond the current batting average, or the one who sees in a restaurant server something more than the way he or she puts the beverages on the table. I like people who see more than meat and potatoes, who continue to be fascinated by the wonderful nuances that make up every day.

In truth, I believe God has endued all of us with this capacity. That's why preschool children so often startle us with out-of-this-world observations. "Where did that come from?" we ask; and I want to answer, "From the way the Creator wired us up." But, as time goes by, a good share of us humans seem to lose that capacity. I read once of a tombstone somewhere that read, "Here lies John Anderson. Born a man, died a grocer." There's nothing wrong with being a grocer, a farmer, a truck driver, a physician, a college professor, or a preacher, but God forbid that any such term should be sufficient to define us. It's tragic, I think, if an executive becomes so efficient at seeing the vaunted bottom line that he can no longer understand the people around him, or if an athlete becomes so absorbed in spiraling a football that he loses his feeling for wife and children and God.

I repeat, God didn't make us this way. God created us as, first of all, persons inhabited by the divine breath and therefore as persons who are not only eternal, but possessed by an instinct for eternity. Unless the culture tampers with our controls, we find it as natural to think about the "big questions" as to breathe. Praying comes naturally to us, as does our sense of awe in the presence of natural wonder and our sense of right and wrong when we see blatant injustice. These responses are part of our original equipment.

But back to our centurion. We know nothing about his background. Odds are that he was Roman and thus easily trusted by the government, though it's possible he came from a province farther away. Almost surely he was part of the career military system; such commitment was essential to gaining the centurion's post. He was no doubt an intelligent man, with some substantial people skills, but he was probably not highly educated in the formal sense of the word. And because his effectiveness depended so much on his knowledge of what was happening in the community where he served, he had heard about Jesus.

So there in Capernaum, he came to Jesus. "Lord, my servant is lying at home paralyzed, in terrible distress" (Matt. 8:6). Jesus knew the centurion was not just making conversation. For one thing, centurions didn't engage in small talk with the general citizenry; and for another, when people spoke to Jesus about any kind of human need, there was an implied request. A statement like the centurion's always ended with an unspoken question: "What are you going to do about this?" Jesus recognized the implied issue; for him it was a commonplace. He replied immediately, "I will come and cure him."

There's something so matter-of-fact about Jesus' statement that it ought to shock and thrill us. Jesus was utterly sure of his ability to deal with the servant's paralysis, and also immediately willing to do so. But the centurion feels he has a problem. "Lord, I am not worthy to have you come under my roof; but only speak the word, and my servant will be healed" (Matt. 8:8).

I think there's more in the centurion's answer than the respect of a soldier for a teacher, even a teacher who performs miracles. After all, the centurion had the power and the legal right to say to Jesus or nearly any other person, "Carry my load the next mile," and the person would have to do so. By the nature of the relationship between a representative of the Roman government and a person in occupied territory, the centurion could couch the exchange as a command, not a request. But this is a sensitive man. He sees some goodness in Jesus that is so out of the ordinary that he is awed and humbled by it. More than that: he is so impressed by Jesus' power that he believes distance is no issue. "Only speak the word." It's almost as if the centurion had a small grasp of the kind of thing the writer of John's Gospel had in mind when he wrote, "In the beginning was the Word. . . . All things came into being through him" (John 1:1, 3). "You are the Word; speak the word."

Let me interrupt myself long enough to say something else about this centurion. It isn't a huge matter, but it's consequential enough to interrupt my story. I like the goodness I see in this centurion. He *cared* about his servant. Cared enough to seek out the Jewish teacher and humbly ask for help. Now a cynic, posing momentarily as a realist, might answer, "What's so great about that? The servant—a slave, probably—is valuable to him, a piece of property. The centurion is nothing more than a tough-minded administrator." And if it weren't for other elements in the story, I would perhaps have to concede this cynic a point. But I think this man's remarkable faith-declaration to Jesus was of a piece with his concern for his servant. I'm not contending that we are fully consistent humans; there is in all of us too much evidence to the contrary. But one can generally trace the strand of godliness that runs through a person's life. If you watched this man worry about his servant and the servant's "terrible distress," you wouldn't be surprised that he would have such utter confidence in Jesus' power and willingness. To put it another way, it's not a long step from the way we treat the table server at the restaurant to the attitude with which we approach God.

I've said that this centurion is a soldier-theologian. The hyphenation is very intentional. His theology and his soldiering are of a piece. When, as a young pastor with two rural congregations in Wisconsin, I heard my people talk about their walk with Christ in the metaphors of plowing, milking, and canning, I knew they were processing their faith through the familiar categories of their daily life— just as, a few years later in Green Bay, Wisconsin, I sometimes heard my football players and their wives expressing their faith-walk in the language of the football field. This is a wonderful two-edged sword: the daily routine, which might otherwise seem common and even tedious, is sanctified; and our Christian walk, which might otherwise be a bit too heavenly minded, now takes on the wonderful smudge and smell of earth and sweat.

See how this soldier reasons through his theological problem. He wants Jesus to heal his servant. Logically, this means a visit from the Great Physician. After all, there's a peculiar power in this Galilean's presence. In our day we'd refer to his "charismatic personality," and we'd no doubt see some psychosomatic factors at work. The first-century world didn't have our vocabulary, but I'm quite sure they operated with many of the same thought patterns. But the centurion has a problem: he can't imagine this holy man entering his home.

I don't know what was wrong with the centurion's home. Did an opulence that had previously made him proud embarrass him when he thought of Jesus coming there? A friend told me how he began to apologize for his very expensive automobile when he hosted a godly, self-sacrificing missionary; suddenly his hypercomfort seemed rather tawdry. Were there pagan images in the soldier's home? Or is it simply that all of life comes into a dramatic reevaluation in the serene presence of our Lord? How exactly would we feel if Jesus stepped into our home, our garage, our den, our office?

Whatever it was (and in truth, Jesus wants to visit us wherever we live and work), the centurion hurriedly explained to Jesus that there was no need for him to come. "For I also am a man under authority, with soldiers under me; and I say to one, 'Go,' and he goes, and to another, 'Come,' and he comes, and to my slave, 'Do this,' and the slave does it" (Matt. 8:9). It was really quite simple. The centurion knew how a chain of command works, and he knew that in the larger chain of command, Jesus had power over sickness. As he saw it, all Jesus needed to do was to say to the servant's paralysis, "Go!" and it would have to leave. It was really very simple.

Jesus was so amazed by the centurion's theology that he was diverted momentarily from his mission of healing. He said to those who were following him, "Truly I tell you, in no one in Israel have I found such faith. I tell you, many will come from east and west and will eat with Abraham and Isaac and Jacob in the kingdom of heaven, while the heirs of the kingdom will be thrown into the outer darkness, where there will be weeping and gnashing of teeth" (Matt. 8:10–12).

Let me pause on the phrase "in no one in Israel." Obviously Jesus included in that number the scribes and Pharisees who came to hear him and to critique his ministry; they were learned men, meticulous theologians, but they didn't have such faith. Nor, if we take Jesus literally, did that very special Pharisee, Nicodemus, who was earnest enough that he would seek out a visit with Jesus, but still be bewildered by the message of the new birth. And come to think of it, Jesus' words must have included even his disciples, those twelve sincere men who had left their daily run in order to be with him. Even they hadn't reduced the theological issues into such concrete, faith-insistent terms. It was this soldier-theologian who looked at sickness and health—and, ultimately, hell and heaven and evil and good—through the lens of his grimy, commonplace, daily business, and saw eternity as clear as crystal.

In case you're wondering, the servant was healed. "In that hour," Matthew tells us. And it was as simple as the centurion's diagnosis: "Go," Jesus had told him; "let it be done for you according to your faith" (Matt. 8:13).

I try to keep my eyes open for soldiers, business people, teachers, novelists, clerks, and table waiters who are theologians. They will tell me some things I never learned in seminary and still haven't found in a library.

Chapter 12

An Obscure Hero

Scripture Reading: John 8:1–11

I like to get near to heroes. They make me feel smaller, which in turn makes me want to grow, to be better. As the years have gone by, I have become more and more choosy about my heroes. This is partly a matter of my age, of course, and I suspect it's also a reaction to the times in which we live. I seem to react badly to those annual lists of the "most admired people" in America, or in the world. I don't admire someone for becoming a popular entertainer or for getting rich or for hitting an extraordinary number of home runs. I may well respect the talent involved in some of these achievements, but I don't see anything heroic about them. My heroes are those persons who demonstrate character, because character doesn't come cheap. It's usually a lifetime enterprise. And here's a wonderful thing about character: though it may grow quietly, often unnoticed, it has a way of showing up just when it is needed most, and particularly when it is most costly to the person who demonstrates it.

So let me tell you about a bona fide hero, a man I wish I could have known at first hand. When by the grace of God I get to heaven, I want to look him up. This might be difficult in any place but heaven, because I don't know the man's name. But I'm satisfied that heaven's computer system will locate him for me in a matter of seconds.

Let me tell you the story. Early one morning, Jesus was teaching in the temple. A sizable crowd had gathered around. Ordinarily Jesus taught outdoors, and by stationing himself in the temple grounds he was inviting trouble. He was a rabbi, with a large following among the common people, but he didn't belong to the rabbinical elite, and the established religious leaders looked on Jesus as something of an intruder. They admired his obvious gifts, and they were impressed by the miracles he performed, but he didn't "belong" to them, and often his teachings offended them—sometimes because they disagreed with the position he was taking and sometimes because he seemed to them to be making presumptuous claims about himself.

So they decided to dispose of him. All they needed was a good case to bring against him. It couldn't be some arcane issue that only a few scholars would recognize; it had to be some instance in which almost anyone could see that he was setting himself against the law of Moses. One day someone in their number was bright enough and devious enough to figure out an effective approach. This might have been a committee development, but the idea was nasty enough that I judge it to be the product of a singularly mean mind.

They knew that Jesus had a penchant for the underdog and the despised. Not only did he associate with such people, he sometimes made them the heroes of his fascinating little stories. So they interrupted his teaching with a woman who, they said, had been taken in adultery—"caught in the very act," they reported.

The scene was quite incongruous: an obviously distinguished body of men, dressed in a manner appropriate to their position in life, dragging a pathetic woman. She may have been beautiful (if Hollywood or television were producing the story, this would be a given), but at this moment it's hard to tell. She's disheveled, she's crying, she's terrified, she's pathetic, clutching to herself whatever remnant of a garment she was able to grab even as she was apprehended.

Before we go farther, I should tell you that this story is disputed among scholars. We usually find it in our Bibles as the opening portion of the eighth chapter of the Gospel of John, but it's also usually accompanied by a footnote. The footnote explains that the very oldest biblical manuscripts lack this portion, that others include it as part of the seventh chapter of John or the twenty-first chapter, or as part of the twenty-first chapter of Luke's Gospel.

Now I think what all of this tells us is this: The story is probably as authentic as a story could be. That's why it appears in these ancient manuscripts in so many different places. It looks as if everyone knew the story and everyone believe it belonged, but they didn't have a place for it, so the early Christian teachers and those who copied the manuscripts fit it in wherever they thought it might be appropriate.

The biblical writer tells us why these distinguished men were bringing this woman to Jesus. They were not really concerned about her sin; they wanted to make a point. Specifically, they hoped to force Jesus to contradict the law of Moses, in order to discredit him. By doing so, they could begin to diminish his popularity and his authority with the people, until they could destroy his following. They were not nice men. They were educated, they were impressively dressed, they were leaders in the community, but they were not nice men. I suspect someone had tipped them off about a man and a woman who were having an adulterous relationship, and they had stationed themselves where they could break in on the couple at a crucially incriminating moment. And of course they were not equal opportunity enforcers. They weren't interested in the man's behavior; all they wanted was the woman. After all, they could understand why a man might engage in adultery, but a woman who did so was much more glamorous, made a much better gossip headline, and of course was much more vulnerable.

So they brought the woman to Jesus. As I said earlier, they didn't really care about her; she was just a pawn in their political/religious game. It was Jesus they were after. The woman was a means to an end. Always watch out for anyone who is willing to use people as a means to an end, no matter what the end is. There is no end so good that people should be exploited to bring it about.

The woman must have been terrified. Not only had she been caught, and humiliated, she was also alone. We don't know if the man deserted her, or if the group let him go or perhaps even insisted that he go. In any event, the one person in the world who ought to have been with the woman in this frightening moment was gone. It's true, as the old saying goes, that misery loves company, but it is never truer than when we're talking about the misery of being caught in our sins.

The woman's captors got right to the point. "Teacher," they said to Jesus (as if they respected him—but more particularly because it was at the point of his teaching that they intended to destroy him), "Teacher, this woman was caught in the very act of committing adultery. Now in the law Moses commanded us to stone such women. Now what do you say?" (John 8:4–5). Let me interrupt the scene long enough to point out that these scholars (now I'm being nasty in my use of this word)—these scholars didn't quote the Bible very well. They said that Moses commanded that such women should be stoned. Here's what the law of Moses said, in Leviticus 20:10: "If a man commits adultery with the wife of his neighbor, both the adulterer and the adulteress shall be put to death." Of course, these men weren't the last to quote the Bible to fit their own prejudices and presuppositions. I suspect that we religious people have done things to the Bible that a run-of-the-mill sinner wouldn't think of doing.

We know what these men had in mind. "They said this," the Gospel tells us, "to test [Jesus], so that they might have some charge to bring against him" (John 8:6). They knew that Jesus spent a good deal of time with the sort of folks they carefully avoided, people easily classified as sinners. They must also have noted that one of the reasons the common folk were so drawn to Jesus was because he seemed understanding of their weaknesses. The accusers were therefore sure they could stumble Jesus into trouble.

Well, I think you're familiar enough with this story to know what Jesus did next. He didn't honor their question with an answer. This must surely have frustrated them, because they couldn't incriminate him unless he said something. Instead, he bent down and wrote with his finger on the ground. We don't know what he wrote; we can only speculate, and I'm sure a legion of novelists, playwrights, and poets have done so. Some say he was just doodling, gaining time while he thought and prayed. Some say he was listing some of the sins of which these accusing men might be guilty. The word the biblical writer used is not the simple word for "write," but the Greek word for "write against"—that is, to make charges against someone. But I repeat, we don't know. As fascinating as it is to exercise our imagination, we have no sure idea what Jesus wrote.

The accusers pressed their accusation. "They kept on questioning him" (John 8:7). At last Jesus "straightened up and said to them, 'Let anyone among you who is without sin be the first to throw a stone at her.'" Having said this, Jesus stooped down and began writing again, like a person who has been interrupted in composing a letter.

Then a strange thing happened. One by one, the accusers slipped away. When the last of them was gone, Jesus—for the first time—spoke to the woman. "Woman, where are they? Has no one condemned you?" (John 8:10). It seems like a courtroom scene in which the judge notes that the prosecuting attorney has collected his or her papers, put them in his attaché case, and left the room. With no one to make a case, the prisoner is free. The woman answered that there was no longer anyone there to accuse her. Jesus spoke a wonderful word of forgiveness and a strategic word of admonition: "Neither do I condemn you. Go your way, and from now on do not sin again" (John 8:11).

That's the end of the story. We never again hear of the woman, or of her accusers. The story illustrates the grace and love that are to be found in Jesus Christ; it also demonstrates his delightful ability to deal with his opponents. But I'm telling you the story because I'm fascinated by the person I consider key to the whole unfolding plot, the one who changed the course of the story. Ponder again what happened. The accusers made their case. The woman clearly is guilty. Except for one sentence, Jesus makes no argument. In a sense, in fact, Jesus authorizes the potential executioners to go ahead. He tells them to start their process of judgment, with a sinless one leading the way. If one is a literalist, only one sinless person has to step forward. Let that person cast the first stone, Jesus says, so after the first one is cast, I can follow. It is a stunning challenge. All that is needed is for one holy hothead to pick up a stone and throw it—some holy hothead with a poor memory, who has forgotten his sinfulness. Or for that matter, some holy person who answers Jesus, "We're not here to talk about our sins, but about hers." That would have been a logical reaction, or else it wouldn't have come so easily to my rationalizing mind.

Instead, as they stood there, one man walked away. And, one by one, the others followed him, until the prosecuting attorneys' bench was empty.

Who was that man who led the way? He fascinates me, because he is the center of the story. The woman is a helpless victim, outnumbered eight or nine or a dozen to one. Jesus is a voice of gracious reason, but he is only one, and as far as the others are concerned he belongs to the opposition party. The key is the person who broke the prosecuting phalanx. The story revolves on him.

And we don't know his name. He has been lost in the obscurity of history. What kind of man was he? What went through his mind that morning? Where did he get the courage to lead the way?

Was it his age? Most translations refer to him as "the oldest." There's logic in that, because in that first-century world a group of people would be inclined to wait to see what the oldest in the group would do. But was it his age that made him do this strong, generous, and unlikely thing? Some people say that we become more generous in our judgments as we grow older. I'd like to believe that, since I'm resolutely becoming part of that older group, but the facts aren't nec-essarily there. A colleague of mine says that as we grow older we become caricatures of ourselves, both physically and in our person-alities. A self-righteous person is likely only to become more self-righteous as the years go by. I doubt that we can find an adequate explanation for this man's action by saying that he had mellowed with age. After all, he was tough enough that he joined this lynching party, so there's no reason to look for sudden mellowness in him.

Did he remember some sin of his past? If so, how come he had a better memory than the other men in the party? Was there in him some sense of fairness that compelled him to wonder why this woman was there and why they weren't also dealing with the man who was equally involved? But if so, how is it that he had this sense of fairness when his comrades in judgment did not? Did he simply examine his own soul? If so, there's nothing "simple" about it. When we humans begin truly to examine our souls, deeply and profoundly, we're doing an unlikely thing, a wonderfully holy thing.

I confess that I don't know what made him act as he did. I only know that I think he was a great man, a true hero. He was a person with convictions about right and wrong. He knew that adultery is a great evil, destructive of home and society, so he opposed it. But with all his convictions, he somehow had room in his heart for grace. It's important to have deep convictions about right and wrong; in truth, such convictions are in short supply in our relativistic age. But the convictions should never be so all-pervasive that they leave no room for grace.

God bless him, this man had the courage to take a lonely stand. He didn't make a speech. As someone who's done a lot of speaking, I can tell you that speech making sometimes becomes a posturing that takes the place of action. And, come to think of it, he didn't ask anyone else to go with him. He simply walked away. As the saying goes, he talked with his feet.

And as he did so, he couldn't have known if anyone would follow him. During those moments before making his fateful decision, he had good reason to think that from this time forward he would be despised by his friends and associates. As a matter of fact, maybe he was. Perhaps, for the rest of his life, he knew that someone in that circle was always saying, "If that fellow hadn't walked out on us, we would have gotten Jesus on the dilemma horns we'd planned. But he walked away." Perhaps when this obscure hero died, there were still such mutterings on the outskirts of discussion returning back from the cemetery.

I'm not telling you he was a perfect man. He probably wouldn't have been in the coterie of judgment that morning if he was. But I insist that he was a great one. He had the courage to take a stand, and in the process he turned the tide. To me, he's a hero. When, by the grace of God, I get to heaven, I want to get near to this man for a while. But I wish I could get near him here. Heroes, you know, are always in short supply.

Chapter 13

"Rock" for a Reason

Scripture Reading: Matthew 16:13–23

*M*ost of us like Simon Peter. I'm not thinking just now of professional theologians or Bible students, or of those in the Catholic tradition who see him as the rock on which the church has been built. I'm thinking rather of the average reader, Protestant, Catholic, or casual nonbeliever; all of us seem drawn to this rugged, outspoken, mercurial fisherman. But I submit that we're drawn to him probably for the wrong reasons—the kind of reasons suggested by the adjectives I've just used in describing him.

It's true that he was a bit of a blunderer. It's also true that he sometimes (perhaps often!) spoke when he should have remained silent. For many of us he is the Patron Saint of Ill-Chosen Words, one we may think of when we leave a conversation muttering to ourselves, "Why did I ever say such a stupid thing?" And worst of all, it's true that he denied his Lord, even after vigorously declaring that he would follow him to the death.

With such a record, all of it in plain view, it's easy to wonder why Jesus chose Peter as one of the Twelve, and, more than that, made him one of the three on whom he most relied. We can wonder also why he would call this person a "rock," "Peter," [*petra*]. At times the name seems so inappropriate one might think Jesus used it playfully, the way schoolboys used to nickname the biggest fellow in the class "Tiny." Did the other apostles sometimes grimace when they heard Jesus call him Peter? I wonder, on some of those occasions when Simon Peter did one of his signature things, if some other disciple poked him in the ribs, grinned, and said, "Way to go, *Rock!*"

I want to say that Jesus named him "Rock" for a reason. See his blunderings, his ill-spoken words, and his denials, but remember that Rock was his name, and that it was no mistake.

Most of us know the major details in Peter's story, but let me review it. Simon was a fisherman on the Sea of Galilee, along with his brother Andrew. As such he was what today we would call a small businessman. Probably most of the men who worked the Sea of Galilee were in that category, because fishing with nets was generally an enterprise for two or more persons. I see him as a naturally popular person, someone always good for a story, an outrageous statement, or a hearty laugh. He was probably neither too good, nor too bad.

And he was a seeker. It seems almost certain that he and his brother Andrew were among those who not only went to hear John the Baptist but either came back as often as possible or even stayed with John for extended periods. In matters of the spirit, he was looking for something more. Andrew—on John the Baptist's recommendation—sought out Jesus first, and when he reported the visit to Simon, it was with the word, "We have found the Messiah" (John 1:41). This is significant, as it indicates that Andrew and Simon—and probably several others in their circle of earnest conversation—were speaking frequently about matters of deepest intent, including the Messiah: When? Where? Who? How?

For centuries a faithful remnant in Israel had looked for the Messiah. I suspect their interests varied all the way from the purely political to the deeply religious. Some probably expected a Messiah with the qualities of a Moses or a David, to wipe out their enemies, while others looked for a prophetic-type figure, who would influence spiritual renewal. I venture further that both found basis for their expectations in the traditions of their people and in their Scriptures.

But the subject took on dramatically new dimensions with the appearance of John the Baptist. Prior to John several political leaders—small-time revolutionaries, some might call them—had appeared on the scene, but John was the first person in perhaps four centuries who carried the aura of a true prophet of God. His persona, his indifference to public approval, and his message stamped him as in the line of Elijah, Isaiah, and Amos. The people's first inclination was to see John himself as the Messiah, but when he vigorously denied that conjecture, he only quickened the public interest. And when he said that his job was to prepare the way for someone immeasurably greater, the seekers had to be on tiptoes of expectation.

We don't know how close Simon Peter was to John the Baptist, but there's no doubt he was among those who had listened to John with high expectation, and with part of their expectation rooted in their longing for the Messiah. When Andrew told Simon, "We have found the Messiah," we can see how much messianic expectation was at the forefront of their daily conversations. Simon Peter was a seeker.

That says a great deal for him, and it also helps us to understand him. Seekers are often an erratic lot. As they go from one cause to another, casting their enthusiasm on first one leader and then another, a more deliberate outsider will eventually conclude they are unstable. Perhaps the very term "stable seeker" is an oxymoron. To be a seeker is to be on the move. I think it's possible to be a cautious seeker (though even here there's a personality clash), but I doubt that one can stand fast and yet be on the search. Let's agree, then, that the very qualities that made Peter a seeker and eventually a leader among the apostles were also qualities that got him into trouble.

If I may, I will compare Simon Peter to his ancestor, Jacob. If you remember the story of Jacob and Esau, you may feel that you would have liked Esau more than Jacob. Jacob's business dealings and even his family relationships were just a little too clever. I'm being charitable when I say that his ethics were marginal. In truth, they were often downright crooked. But one thing had to be said for Jacob: he knew what was worth going after, and he pursued it passionately. He recognized that the birthright and, later, his father's blessing were more than financial considerations; they were part of the holy heritage of his people. There was a spiritual quality in Jacob that Esau didn't demonstrate until much later in his life. Jacob exercised his spiritual hunger in ways we can't condone, but his hunger itself was admirable. And so it was with Peter, the seeker.

That hunger and Peter's readiness to assume leadership even when unsought made him join the early followers of Jesus. We don't know how many disciples Jesus had when he chose the Twelve. It may have been a fairly large number; after all, a little later Jesus sent out seventy other followers, and even they were no doubt drawn from a larger group. To be one of such a select group had to bless Peter's ego. Many people spend their days in relative obscurity even while they dream of advancement and significance. Now Peter had it. Not only was he chosen by the fascinating young rabbi, but the teacher even came to Peter's home.

And far more. The teacher called him the Rock. If Peter acted before his call anything like the way he did afterward, "rock" was not the definitive name for his personality type.

Nevertheless, Jesus moved him up in the ranks. Among the Twelve, three men stood out: Simon Peter and the sons of Zebedee, James and John. Before long, when there were occasions of special spiritual significance or need, Jesus called on these three to lead the way with him. For instance, when it was clear that the daughter of Jairus, a leader in a synagogue, had died even while Jesus and the disciples were on the way to pray for her, Jesus "allowed no one to follow him" into the death chamber "except Peter, James, and John" (Mark 5:37–40). And there was the time when Jesus took this same trio with him "up a high mountain apart, by themselves" (Mark 9:2). On this occasion they saw their Lord "transfigured before them" and engaged in a conversation with Elijah and Moses, who had been dead for centuries. Again when Jesus went alone to pray on the night of his betrayal and trial, he asked these three to watch with him and to "keep awake" (Mark 14:33–34). It is quite clear that Jesus saw a unique capacity in these three men that didn't exist in the same measure or depth with the others; thus, when Jesus was at a point where he wanted someone on whom to lean, he turned to these three.

Sometimes Peter was magnificent. The most notable instance was the day Jesus questioned his disciples about how the people were evaluating his ministry. After they had reported, Jesus made the question personal: "But who do you say that I am?" (Matt. 16:15). I sense that silence consumed the group for extended seconds. Without a doubt this very question had become a primary topic of discussion among the disciples; until now it seemed that little else mattered. Nevertheless, it's a long leap from private speculation to public declaration.

Unless your name is Simon Peter. He broke the silence with no preamble, no qualifying provisions, and no uncertainty. "You are the Messiah, the Son of the living God" (Matt. 16:16). And just as quickly Jesus answered. "Blessed are you, Simon son of Jonah! For flesh and blood has not revealed this to you, but my Father in heaven" (Matt. 16:17).

Something about Peter's statement was very special. Others had made almost identical statements. Remember, this is the way Peter's brother Andrew first encouraged Simon to come and meet Jesus: "We have found the Messiah" (John 1:41). John the Baptist's introduction of Jesus surely implied that he was the Messiah. When the woman of Samaria told her neighbors of her encounter with Jesus, it was with the question, "He cannot be the Messiah, can he?" (John 4:29)—surely a rhetorical question. And when Martha and Jesus conferred after Lazarus's death, Martha declared, "I believe that you are the Messiah, the Son of God, the one coming into the world" (John 11:27). From these instances I think it is fair to assume that a great many people were saying just what Peter said—some of them cautiously, and some of them with more hope than conviction. But I'm altogether sure people were saying just what Peter said that day. Still, when Peter said it, Jesus hailed his statement as a message from the Father.

But almost as quickly as Peter received recognition as a spokesperson for heaven, he was discredited as a representative of the enemy. Jesus explained to his disciples that he was going to Jerusalem to be abused and killed, but then again to rise from the dead. Peter seemed to hear only the first part of the story—or perhaps couldn't comprehend the "rising again" idea. He "began to rebuke [Jesus], saying, 'God forbid it, Lord! This must never happen to you.'" Jesus, in turn, said to Peter, "Get behind me, Satan! You are a stumbling block to me; for you are setting your mind not on divine things but on human things" (Matt. 16:22–23).

How can one go so easily from angelic to demonic talk? Unfortunately, it's not at all difficult. I'm no Simon Peter, so my contrasts aren't so dramatic and are surely not so significant, but I've been startled at times by my ability to go from beauty to ugliness. And I don't want to pretend exceptional knowledge of Peter's spiritual state, but it's probably clear that we are most susceptible to spiritual ineptitude soon after an experience of spiritual exaltation. In general, it's hard to keep our spiritual equilibrium when someone—whether God or an overly enthusiastic friend—tells us how wonderful we are. And of course the danger is especially great for those of us who feel obligated to offer our opinion even when it is not sought.

This happened to Peter again not many days later, though in this instance no great harm was done. This was the occasion when Jesus took Peter, James, and John to "a high mountain," where they were privy to a conversation between Jesus, Moses, and Elijah. It was an astonishing experience, the kind that would cause most of us to say, "I was struck dumb." Not Peter. He said, "Rabbi, it is good for us to be here; let us make three dwellings, one for you, one for Moses, and one for Elijah" (Mark 9:5). As spur-of-the-moment comments go, Peter hadn't done too badly. But it was vintage Peter; as Mark puts it, "He [Peter] did not know what to say, for they were terrified" (Mark 9:6). Some people, not knowing what to say, will remain silent. Peter, in the same predicament, found something to say. He seemed always to feel that an embarrassing word was to be preferred to an embarrassing silence.

Peter's darkest hour also had to do with inappropriate speech. As Jesus and the disciples concluded the meal we now call "the Last Supper," Jesus warned the disciples that they would all desert him. Of course, Peter spoke up. At such a time, you or I might have too; or perhaps more likely we would have poked the person next to us, muttering: "Don't just stand there. Say something." Peter said, "Even though all become deserters, I will not" (Mark 14:29). It was an especially unfortunate statement, since it was not simply a declaration of personal loyalty, but one that chose to make its emphasis on the predicted failure of others. Jesus then went on to say that before the cock crowed twice, Peter would deny him three times. Peter became vehement, promising that he would die with Jesus if necessary—and the others "said the same" (Mark 14:31).

As you probably know, Peter did indeed deny his Lord three times. I'm inclined to think that if Peter hadn't made such extravagant statements, he would simply have fled to a safe distance where he wouldn't have been put at such peril. Instead, he stayed close enough to see what was going on. It was an act of loyalty to do so. But each time he had the opportunity to enforce his loyalty Peter's heart failed him, so that rather than following through on whatever brave intentions he had he made the matter tragically worse. With the cock's crow, Peter "broke down and wept" (Mark 14:72). Humiliation, self-despising, repentance—probably these and many other emotions were mixed in Peter's tears.

So much more could be said about Peter. He was one of the disciples who came to the empty tomb after Mary Magdalene reported her experience. Some days later it was Peter who led six other disciples on a fishing trip that was an embarrassing futility until Jesus turned it into a miracle. It was at this occasion, too, that Simon Peter hinted of some of his continuing wrestling with jealousy and issues of position. When Jesus pressed him for a full statement of love, Peter "saw the disciple whom Jesus loved," and asked, "Lord, what about him?" (John 21:20–21). Jesus' answer was a bit of a rebuke: "If it is my will that he remain until I come, what is that to you? Follow me!" (John 21:22).

And Peter did just that. On the Day of Pentecost it was Peter who dared to stand before the crowd and make what could perhaps be called the first Christian sermon. This time there was no fear: "Therefore let the entire house of Israel know with certainty that God has made him both Lord and Messiah, this Jesus whom you crucified" (Acts 2:36). It was Peter, some days later, who dared to tell the esteemed religious leaders of Israel that he and John were acting in "the name of Jesus Christ of Nazareth, whom you crucified, whom God raised from the dead," and to insist that there was "salvation in no one else" (Acts 4:10,12).

It was Peter, too, who confronted sin in the fledgling body of the church in the instance of Ananias and Sapphira, and he was the instrument of God's purposes in an early opening of the door to the Gentile world, when he brought the gospel to Cornelius and his household—and then in pleading the cause of the Gentiles before his fellow leaders of the church in Jerusalem. Not long after that, Peter essentially disappears from the story in the Acts of the Apostles, as Paul becomes the key figure. But tradition makes Peter the leader of the church in Rome (an unlikely appointment, one might say—the rugged fisherman as the lead personality for the capital of the majestic Roman Empire!). But that's Peter for you. He's really quite unpredictable.

Tradition also says that at the time of Peter's martyrdom the authorities first crucified Peter's wife as they compelled him to look on; and that when it was time for his own execution, Peter was adamant that he must be crucified with his head down, because he wasn't worthy to die as his Lord had died. The story may be legend, but there's a certain ring of truth about it.

But back to the question I raised earlier. Why did Jesus call him a "rock," this man who seemed so often the essence of instability? And why did our Lord place such trust in him, and find in his declaration of faith a quality unlike any other?

You could answer that this is God's business, and none of mine; God chooses whom he will and that's enough—and you'd have a point. But I can't help asking the question, and even daring to offer some answers. For one, as I mentioned earlier, Simon Peter was a seeker. That's a holy quality. The Scriptures show God constantly seeking after us, so there's something especially right about our turning and seeking after God.

I'm impressed, too, that Peter always had the faith to *try*. When Jesus walked on the Sea of Galilee, it was Peter who decided he should follow his Lord in such a miraculous venture. He sank, but he tried. In truth, I'm not sure Peter's intentions in trying were all good, but as one of those people who would rather others take the venturesome lead, I doff my hat to a fellow who will step out of the boat, regardless of his motivations.

And, yes, Peter talked too much, with too little thought. But he wasn't afraid to speak. The very audacity that sometimes resulted in his making a fool of himself was the very audacity that caused him to witness fearlessly on the Day of Pentecost, and later before a body of learned men who might easily and rightly have intimidated him.

But especially, remember this: he never gave up on himself. He had reason to. He stumbled so many times. He denied the finest fact of his life, his relationship to Jesus of Nazareth. He fell asleep when his Master had pleaded for his help in prayer. He insulted his colleagues by announcing the superiority of his loyalty to theirs, then failed more ignominiously than all of them. But he never gave up on himself. It goes without saying that our Lord never gave up on Simon Peter, but that isn't enough. There is a point at which we simply must not give up on ourselves.

That's the stuff a rock is made of. Ask Peter. And ask the Lord who gave him the name. He had his reasons.

Chapter 14

Young Man in a Hurry

Scripture Reading: Acts 12:6–12

*T*he most important book in the world." That's the way the late William Barclay, one of the most popular biblical scholars of the twentieth century, described the Gospel of Mark.[1] Barclay dared that extravagant statement because most scholars agree that Mark's Gospel was the first of the four Gospels to be written, and thus the first life of Jesus in our possession. A great many scholars also feel that the persons who wrote the Gospels of Matthew and Luke proba- bly had Mark's Gospel in hand as they wrote. When you consider that more books have been written about Jesus than about any other per- son that ever walked our planet, and that literally every day an unknown number of persons in the world are working on new books regarding Jesus, his life, and his teachings, you have to agree that Mark started quite a publishing enterprise.

He had a good base for doing so. He heard the story told by Paul and Barnabas. He was perhaps still in his teens or at most in his early twenties when he sat in on their white-hot presentations of the faith. For Mark, it was the stuff of evangelism, shared often under perilous circumstances to street corner gatherings in Asia Minor (and later in Rome), whispered in secret home gatherings of new believers, dis- cussed with passing philosophers who heard it skeptically. Mark was getting a graduate education in residence with the first theologian of the Christian faith, Paul, and with the person I think of as the premier exemplar of the faith, Barnabas. It's hard to improve on being part of such a daily, living seminar.

But there's still more to be said. The early church generally agreed

95

that the person who wrote the Gospel of Mark was speaking for Peter, the prince of the apostles. Papias (ca. 60–130), the bishop of Hierapolis; Clement of Alexandria (ca. 150–215); and the scholar Origen (ca. 185–254) all testified to Mark's unique role as Peter's interpreter. Clement said that Mark wrote his Gospel at the request of those who knew he had followed Peter "for a long time," and that he "remembered well" what Peter had said. Origen felt Peter had instructed Mark to write this Gospel. I'm quite sure that if Mark had titled the book he wrote, he would have named it "The Gospel According to Peter," not the Gospel of Mark.

So who was this Mark, the student of Paul and Barnabas, and Peter's confidant? Putting his story together is a bit of a detective enterprise. The pieces of the story are easily found, but joining them together sometimes involves some circumstantial handling. I want to be utterly honest with you in this matter, but I don't want you to lose the wonder of it all, because in my mind Mark makes what we sometimes call a whopping good story.

Spiritually speaking, he came from good stock. His mother, Mary, was one of the faithful band of women who contributed to the work of Jesus. She must have been a person of some means, because it was in her home that many of the followers of Jesus gathered for prayer after Peter had been imprisoned, in the earliest days of the fledgling Christian movement. It's interesting that the book of Acts describes it this way: "the house of Mary, the mother of John whose other name was Mark" (Acts 12:12). Many Bible students feel that it was in this home that Jesus and his disciples met for the Last Supper.

All of which indicates that young John Mark grew up in the faith and with the faith; and probably also that he grew up with some measure of economic privilege. If his home was large enough that a sizable number of believers could meet there, it was not a residence for a poor or a working-class family. And if Mary was one of the women who helped support Jesus and the disciples in their travels, she had to have some economic substance.

We know not a thing about Mark's father. It seems more than likely that Mary was a widow. Clearly, she was a strong personality, strong enough that she could take the lead in making her home a meeting place for believers. When one considers the peril involved in following Jesus those days (at the time reported in Acts 12 when believers gathered in Mary's home, James had already been executed for his faith and Peter was in prison), one has to conclude that John Mark's mother was one courageous lady. To make her home a haven for the movement was to defy both the Jewish religious authorities and the Roman government. Mary was made of tough stuff. If bloodline plays any part in making us what we are, John Mark was a spiritual thoroughbred.

Now we come to a point where I ask you to venture a guess with me. Tom Wright, Bishop of Durham in the Church of England and surely one of the finest biblical scholars in our time, calls what I am about to say "a quite reasonable guess," even though "it's impossible to prove it."[2] It comes from the night when Jesus met with his disciples for the last time before his betrayal, trial, and crucifixion. When the meal was over, Jesus took his disciples with him to Gethsemane, so that he might pray. Shortly after, when Jesus was arrested, the Gospel of Mark reports that all of Jesus' disciples "deserted him and fled." Then it adds a peculiar little vignette: "A certain young man was following him, wearing nothing but a linen cloth. They [the soldiers] caught hold of him, but he left the linen cloth and ran off naked" (Mark 14:51–52).

Who is this "young man," and why does the Gospel writer bother to tell of the incident? A twenty-first-century reporter might include such a detail for purposes of color, but that can hardly be the reason here. The story of Jesus' betrayal and arrest is unfolding with such poignancy and power that this apparently insignificant detail could seem intrusive at best, if not downright inappropriate. Why is it here?

To go back to the language of Bishop Wright, it's "a quite reasonable guess" that the young man was John Mark. William Barclay says it more emphatically: "By far the most probable answer is that the young man was no other than Mark himself, and that this is his way of saying, 'I was there,' without mentioning his own name at all."[3] I like to see this little incident as Mark's signature to the book, the way a film director may include himself or herself in a crowd scene, or the way the great caricaturist Albert Hirschfeld always hid the name of his daughter, Nina, somewhere in his sketches.

It's easy to imagine the little drama, especially if there's truth in the tradition that the Last Supper convened in the home of Mary, John Mark's mother. The "certain young man" would probably be a young teenager, since in that world a boy was considered a man at age twelve or thirteen, qualified to become a member of the adult religious community. Teenagers are drawn to excitement, and often lack a proper sense of fear. I can see the boy wrapping himself in his sheet so he can hide in a corner just outside the room where Jesus and the disciples are meeting. When they leave the house for Gethsemane, he trails them at a safe distance, unseen in the dark. If so, he is the witness for Jesus' agonizing prayer and the reprimand delivered to the three disciples who fall asleep when they're supposed to be watching with Jesus.

When Jesus is apprehended by Roman soldiers, the disciples flee. But an adventuresome boy isn't going to run, because he wants in on the action. So he follows as the soldiers lead Jesus away, gradually getting closer, to be sure he doesn't miss anything. Suddenly one of the soldiers sees him, grabs at the boy, and gets hold of the sheet the boy is holding to himself. Now the boy wants freedom more than covering. He lets go the sheet and runs from the scene, naked. He's a young man in a hurry; and if indeed he is John Mark, he continues to be in a hurry the rest of his life.

We say this because if there is any characteristic that characterizes Mark's Gospel, it's the sense of hurry. If the vignette to which we've just referred is not the author's signature, his theme word is surely the Greek word *euthus*, a word that is translated "straightway," "forthwith," "immediately," or "instantly." It appears nine times in just the first chapter of the book. It's as if the author is so much on the run that everything he writes is at the same frenetic pace. We're told that this Gospel was intended originally for a Roman audience. That's easy to believe. The Romans were the premier administrators of their day, a people who could build an empire, provide it with roads, bridges, and aqueducts, and keep it remarkably under control. A succinct, quick-read book was just right for them, and John Mark was just the person to write it.

But if Mark's journey was fast, it was also uneven. As we mentioned earlier, he became part of the missionary team of Paul and Barnabas—or Barnabas and Saul, as it was known at first. Along the way, in Pamphilia, Mark "left them and returned to Jerusalem" (Acts 13:13). At that point in the story, the author of Acts makes no comment, but a little later in the story he says that John Mark had "deserted them in Pamphilia" (Acts 15:38).

We have no sure idea why Mark left Paul and Barnabas. The great Chrysostom (ca. 347-407) said that the boy wanted his mother. That's altogether possible, and all the more so because his mother was such a strong woman. At this point he may still have been very dependent on her courage and vigor. Life with Paul and Barnabas had to be rigorous, not at all like home. The older men were absorbed in their mission, a mission that was probably not yet that compelling for young Mark. So he went back home.

But he could have left Paul and Barnabas for quite other reasons. One of the burdens of being young is that the rest of the world moves so slowly, so deliberately, and with such uncertain enthusiasm. When one is eighteen or twenty, it's hard to put up with such tedium. You don't have to accept my earlier opinion that John Mark was the young man who left the scene of Jesus' arrest in cloaked anonymity, or perhaps more accurately, in uncloaked anonymity. Just make him any fairly typical young person who is compelled to work with two older men. The young don't enjoy being junior partners for very long, with their gifts generally unrecognized. And while it seems to me that Barnabas and Paul were a very adventuresome pair involved in an exciting and often perilous enterprise, Mark may have chafed at their fussy style, and perhaps even more that they made their plans without seeking his counsel. You may feel that I am projecting our twenty-first-century mind-set—especially as it reflects the young—on a very different world, and of course you have a point. But, in truth, humans haven't changed that much. The young almost always tend to be impatient with their elders. It's the kind of juice that flows in their veins. Anyway, John Mark left.

Tradition says that in time he went to Egypt and founded the church in Alexandria. And of course eventually he got to Rome, where his life is linked so closely with that of Simon Peter. When Paul is in prison in Rome, he tells the church in Colossae that Mark is there; and "if he comes to you," Paul writes, "welcome him" (Col. 4:10). The young man who was once persona non grata to Paul has

once again become Paul's associate, to whom Paul gives an unso-
licited letter of recommendation.

Along the way, John Mark writes a Gospel. Papias, in the late second century, said that Mark wrote down accurately what he had
learned from Peter. What a pair they had to be! If I'm right in calling
John Mark a young man in a hurry, I think you'll agree that he found
a kindred spirit in the great apostle. Peter rarely wasted time formu-
lating his opinions; they were meant to be expressed now and con-
templated later. Peter might have been one of the few persons in an
older generation who would not too much frustrate the young.

But of course Peter wasn't Mark's only source. A boy growing up
in a home such as his had to have heard endless first- and secondhand
reports of Jesus' teaching and miracles. Thanks to archaeological
studies and growing knowledge of the first-century world, we're
always learning more about the world in which the Gospels were
written, so of course any statement about the Gospels is open to revi-
sion. But what William Barclay wrote a generation ago is still worth
quoting: "Mark is the nearest approach we will ever possess to an eye-
witness account of the life of Jesus."[4]

And I repeat, it's the report of a young man in a hurry—or perhaps
a middle-aged man who has never stopped hurrying. So where
Matthew and Luke begin with stories of Jesus' birth, and where John
begins his Gospel with a theological tour de force, Mark plunges right
into action. After a statement that is essentially a title page, Mark
quotes the prophet Isaiah by way of introducing John the Baptist, who
in turn introduces Jesus—thirty years old and ready to embark on his
eternal mission. As Eugene H. Peterson puts it in introductory
remarks for his translation of Mark's Gospel, "There's an air of
breathless excitement in nearly every sentence he writes."[5] When
your news is as good as what Mark is about to deliver, you have every
reason to be in a hurry.

I'm no longer a young man, but I still remember the delicious
impatience of youth. In truth, I'm embarrassed to recall some of my
audacity. I was a boy of eleven or twelve and so confident of my call
to the ministry that I told my pastor one summer Sunday morning that
if he felt he needed a Sunday off that summer, I would be glad to
preach for him. I remember that he smiled, and I realize now that

when he got home and told his wife, he no doubt laughed out loud.

As I said, this memory embarrasses me, and perhaps I tell it partly as an act of penance. But at the same time I wish I could stir up a small measure of that youthful audacity to flavor my current reticence.

And I wish the church as a whole could do so. The church that I know best, in America and in the Western world, is suffering from middle age or more. We're still quite ready to give advice and to recommend caution, but if we're to sound like John Mark and the grand generation or two of which he was a part, we'll have to go to some churches in Africa or South America or perhaps Korea. Their disposition is still to run; they're in a hurry. I remember a meeting of the executive committee of a world denominational body. The delegates from South Korea introduced a plan for vigorous evangelism. The delegates from several Western countries quickly introduced caution that kept the plan from starting.

I know, I know: If I were in Africa, where converts to Christ number in the thousands weekly, I would be uneasy with some of the ways things are done. I would worry that they're erecting a makeshift building with questionable materials on a shaky foundation. And yet I think, even in my present age, that it would be fun to be part of a movement where a young man in a hurry flees, careless of the sheet he leaves behind.

Chapter 15

A Rare Friend

Scripture Lesson: 2 Timothy 1:15–17

I've never known a boy or a man named Onesiphorus, and I probably never will. Someone now will want to tell me that no one should be saddled with a name so hard to pronounce, but if you'll think for a moment, you'll be able to make a list of contemporary names that are equally difficult for the tongue—or that would be if they weren't already familiar to us.

Perhaps the absence of Onesiphorus is because he hasn't gotten much press; after all, he has only one full paragraph in the New Testament and one other passing reference. But I can find kings in the Old Testament with shorter biographical references; and in more substantive matters of measure we would have a relatively short list of persons who have received as good a report as Onesiphorus. His biography may be short, but it's all positive, and it's wonderfully specific. I doubt that you'll be ready to name a son Onesiphorus after reading what I have to say; and, to be honest, I might take a deep breath if I were told that I'm to have a grandson with this name. No matter; Onesiphorus is one of history's great souls, and he was the kind of friend every one of us would love to claim.

He was a friend to the apostle Paul, and between you and me, I think it wasn't always easy to be Paul's friend. Mind you, Paul is one of my favorite people, and I like even now, at a distance of nearly twenty centuries, to think of him as my friend. But real, close-up friendship with Paul had to be difficult at times. Paul was an exceedingly strong personality with a number of square corners. He had great compassion and a surprising readiness to hear the thinking of others, but he was also ready to go to the mat on any number of issues.

And like almost anyone who works with fierce intensity and who pours huge amounts of energy and emotion into his life and relationships, Paul was inclined at times to self-pity. You can work self-sacrificially for only so long before it occurs to you that probably no one else in the world is working this hard and therefore no one realizes how much you're doing; and at such a point all kinds of unworthy emotions slip into one's mind and out of one's mouth or pen.

I think it's at such a time that Paul pays his tribute to Onesiphorus. Paul is in prison. We don't know the exact circumstances or time, because some elements in this letter don't fit easily into the chronology of Paul's ministry. The letter has a distinct valedictory quality, as if the writer feels it may be the last he will write: "As for me, I am already being poured out as a libation, and the time of my departure has come. I have fought the good fight, I have finished the race, I have kept the faith. From now on there is reserved for me the crown of righteousness" (2 Tim. 4:6–8). This is a tired marathoner, whose eyes are fixed on the finish line. That's the mood of this letter, and it's in such an emotional context that Paul mentions Onesiphorus.

"You are aware," he writes, "that all who are in Asia have turned away from me, including Phygelus and Hermogenes" (2 Tim. 1:15). This sentence reminds me of the Old Testament prophet Elijah, when he complains to God, "I alone am left, and they are seeking my life, to take it away" (1 Kings 19:14). Paul is especially stung by the abdication of Phygelus and Hermogenes, names that are otherwise unknown to us, but who at that moment seem especially significant to Paul. They may not have been part of the first team, but they're among the best backups, so their departure leaves Paul feeling especially vulnerable. We learn later in this letter that Demas, a rather significant aide, has also jumped ship, and that several others had simply gone to other places of ministry, perhaps even at Paul's urging. With it all, Paul feels very much alone. Today, twenty centuries removed, we look at Paul's imprisonments as a badge of honor; at times he had felt that way himself (Acts 28:20). But by now the apostle had spent too much time in prison to romanticize it or even fully to sanctify it.

In the midst of all that is so negative—prison, weariness, a sense of forsakenness, loneliness—Paul remembers Onesiphorus. "May the Lord grant mercy to the household of Onesiphorus, because he often refreshed me and was not ashamed of my chain; when he arrived in Rome, he eagerly searched for me and found me—may the Lord grant that he will find mercy from the Lord on that day! And you know very well how much service he rendered in Ephesus" (2 Tim. 1:15–18).

When it comes to specifics about Onesiphorus, we can only speculate. We know that his name means "useful," or "bringing profit." We don't know of course whether this was the name his parents gave him at birth with a sense of faith, hope, and expectancy, or whether it is a name that was attached to him later in life out of respect for the kind of person he was. Whatever, the name fit. Some scholars feel that since Paul prayed for "mercy to the household of Onesiphorus" that he was dead by the time Paul wrote this letter. Some go on to suggest that he may have been martyred for his friendship with Paul, though that's probably stretching a point. It seems to me that the reference to his household might suggest that Paul had enjoyed hospitality there, and meant by his greeting to indicate his regard for the whole family, or that perhaps the church met in Onesiphorus's house.

Almost surely Onesiphorus was a leader in the church at Ephesus, one of the leading churches in its own right, but strategic in that Ephesus was the capital city for that section of Asia Minor that the New Testament calls "Asia." We don't know what Onesiphorus did for Paul in Ephesus, but it was significant enough that Paul could write to Timothy that "you know very well how much service he rendered" (2 Tim. 1:18). Now that many in that area were turning away from Paul, the contrast with Onesiphorus was dramatic.

But what really mattered to Paul was the depth and quality of the man's friendship. "He often refreshed me," Paul said. Paul used a word that has a root in the idea of *cooling*, which is no doubt an apt picture of "refresh" in that Middle Eastern climate in days long before any kind of air-conditioning.

I've known people like that, and I hope you have too. They're the kind of people whose voice on the telephone or whose return address on e-mail or standard mail is always welcome. I've sometimes noticed that when a secretary says, "You have a call from . . . ," when some names are mentioned I smile even as I pick up the receiver. I'm refreshed at the very prospect of the conversation. What a gift are such friends! Perhaps someday some aspiring medical research specialist will make a study of the effect such persons have on our longevity. If they're ever able to quantify the measurement, I'm certain they'll find that refreshing people add more years to our lives than jogging, whole grain cereals, or any neatly packaged vitamin.

When I speak of people who make us smile, I'm sure you understand that I mean more than simply someone with a good sense of humor. I prize good humor because I enjoy laughing, but I understand what the apostle was driving at in another place when he urged, "Rejoice with those who rejoice, weep with those who weep" (Rom. 12:15). Sometimes the most refreshing word is an arm around the shoulder or a gentle poke in the chest. And sometimes tears, too. I'm often struck by the number of three-hundred-pound tears one sees at the end of a football game, especially at the college level, but sometimes also in the National Football League.

Onesiphorus's ability to refresh was at its best when Paul's circumstances were at their worst. He "was not ashamed of my chain," Paul wrote. We can read several things into Paul's statement. I suspect that some believers distanced themselves from Paul's imprisonments because they felt he wouldn't be in trouble so often if he were only more circumspect in some of his comments. Others no doubt reasoned that if Paul were thrown in prison for his beliefs, anyone too closely associated with him might be in danger of the same fate. For still others it may have been nothing more than our peculiar human uneasiness with people in trouble. Persons with experiences as diverse as a divorce, a malignancy, or a son or a daughter in trouble have told me that their friends often seem to avoid them; and in the same vein, I've often heard people say, "Jim's in trouble and I know I should visit him, but I just don't know what to say."

Whatever the reasons, many people were ashamed of Paul's imprisonment. So much so that early in this letter Paul appeals to his son in the faith, Timothy; "Do not be ashamed . . . of me [our Lord's] prisoner" (2 Tim. 1:8). This shame was spreading through the circle of Paul's associates like a bad infection, with proportions so great that even the most loyal might be taken in.

But not Onesiphorus! We don't know what brought him to Rome, where Paul was jailed, but when he arrived there "he eagerly searched for me and found me" (2 Tim. 1:17). The footnote in your Bible may indicate that the word "eagerly" could also be translated "promptly." I suspect it's possible to be prompt without being eager, but I don't think one can be eager without being prompt. If I were a moviemaker, I would like to portray Onesiphorus's search through the narrow, crowded streets of Rome, into dissolute neighborhoods, inquiring of soldiers on the one hand and of marginal street characters on the other, hoping to find the prison where Paul might be chained. It would be a lonely Paul when he was found, because others who knew the way to Paul's prison were carefully avoiding it.

Life has so many prisons. Richard Lovelace, the seventeenth-century English poet, wrote from prison, "Stone walls do not a prison make, / Nor iron bars a cage," to assure his Althea that his love for her could not be stopped by imprisonment. But the opposite of Lovelace's words is also true. We can be imprisoned without bars, walls, or chains. I dare think that no one will ever read this book who has not spent time in prison. In my years as a pastor I learned that for many people a nursing facility is a prison. The conditions may be sanitary and the care more than adequate, but the institutional feeling is more than some can handle. A job is like that for some people; its economic security is also its bars and chain.

And I venture that for every person officially incarcerated there are five persons who are imprisoned in loneliness, or self-loathing, or stinging memories. Or, for that matter, in beautiful memories. On my first Sunday in a new parish one woman introduced herself after the service by giving me her name and telling me how much she missed her husband. When I visited her some weeks later, I learned that she had been widowed for ten years. She was healthy, busy, and well-read, but imprisoned by the memory of a man she had loved dearly. When a man asked me, "Do you have any idea how lonely I am?" I knew the height of his prison walls. When an interviewer asked a man of considerable professional achievement about a son who had taken his own life nearly two decades before, the man became somber. "Not a day goes by that I don't think of him and of his death." I know some people who are imprisoned by their dreams.

No success replaces what they long ago thought they might someday do and become.

I'm trying to say that some days when you're listening to a friend—or even just an acquaintance—at lunch, or after a meeting, or on an airplane, you may be visiting someone in prison. So many people hurrying about are as behind bars as was Paul when Onesiphorus visited him. If the friend is close enough or the relationship is such that you visit often, you may well grow weary of these prison talks. If so, try making Onesiphorus your patron saint.

The greatest thing about Onesiphorus is that he moved right into Paul's prison. Not as a permanent inhabitant, of course, but as someone who cared enough to hunt until he found Paul and who then "refreshed" him. Did they laugh together? I'm sure of it. Did they pray, and sing hymns? Without a doubt, and perhaps off-key. Did they ponder what the future might hold? Often, but always with an assurance about the ultimate purposes of God and their place in God's purposes.

I have particular regard for Onesiphorus because I've been in prison, and I have been blessed by those who visited me. I think I've had such prison visitors for as far back as I can remember, because we suffer prison terms of one sort or another from our earliest times. Perhaps nothing is more important to our future well-being than the way a parent or grandparent or caretaker attends to us in the prison experience of the first year or two of our lives. We don't remember these attentions intellectually, but our psyche holds to them fiercely.

And so it is through all our years. A grade-school softball game when you dropped a fly ball—a microcosm of losing the World Series—and then a friend put his arm around you when you left the field. The man who, with hardly a word, gripped your hand hard when your mother died. The person you knew you could call when you got a promotion (success is such a peculiar prison because you want so much for someone to rejoice with you and you're not sure who will take the news with what it means to you). And those people who have understood when you were desperately lonely, beaten by self-despising, or bewildered by your own complexity: what great souls they are, what wonderful, clumsy, beautiful angels!

I submit that the worst thing about Paul's prison experience at the time of his writing was the feeling that he was being forsaken. Prison was no new experience for Paul. He wrote his letter to the people at Philippi, his epistle of joy, while he was in prison. Paul was tough; he could take almost anything and thrust it off like the poisonous viper that attached itself to him on the Island of Malta (Acts 28:3–6). But this prison time was different—partly because he was older, partly because he sensed the end might be near, but especially because people he counted on had either turned from him or forgotten him (and at times, one can't tell the difference between the two).

But then there was Onesiphorus! Here was a man who would eagerly search for him, and, finding his prison, treat it as if it were a palace. And he *refreshed* him! He was that cup of spring water on a blistering day.

Thank God for every Onesiphorus. When one visits you, remember his ancient ancestry in Ephesus. And when you have the opportunity, become for someone a member of Onesiphorus's household.

Chapter 16

"A Gardener among Human Beings"

Scripture Reading: Acts 11:19–26

*P*eople who know me even a little will wonder how I dare choose gardening as a figure of speech. To my shame I confess that I recognize only half a dozen flowers by name, and I have never seriously worked at a garden, not even for a full day. I love to see what other people do with flowers and other plants, and I'm always fascinated that while American suburbanites insist on half an acre or more to make a yard like a putting green, the British manage to turn a few square feet into a medley of flowers.

But my particular fascination is with a very special kind of gardener, the kind Katharine Butler Hathaway described in her remarkable book *The Little Locksmith*. As a five-year-old girl, Katharine contracted spinal tuberculosis; she spent most of her growing-up years strapped to a board that was meant to save her from becoming a hunchback. The treatment failed, however. Bright and talented and creative as she was, when Katharine was able to enroll at Radcliffe, she knew that she was "shy and countrified" and the product of an "unfashionable school." But there, in wonderful providence, she was assigned a senior girl, Catharine Huntingdon, who was to be her student mentor.

Catharine Huntingdon was "beautiful and distinguished and talented"; but far more important, she was what Katharine Hathaway called "a gardener among human beings." There are very few such persons, Hathaway said, "and consequently most of the more difficult human plants are all in wrong places, suffering drought, or heat, or dampness, when if only a noticing, intuitive hand could move among them, they might all flourish as they were meant to do."[1]

I want to nominate Barnabas, a sometimes overlooked New Testament personality, as one of the greatest such gardeners of all time. And in saying this, I suspect I am also nominating him as one of the greatest of all Christians.

I should begin by telling you that Barnabas was this man's nickname. His given name was Joseph, but the early Christians soon forgot that, and so have we, so that if I had told you his story under his real name, you'd have no idea of the person I'm talking about.

The New Testament introduces him to us rather early in the book of Acts, back in the days when the believers were so open in their faith that "no one claimed private ownership of any possessions, but everything they owned was held in common" (Acts 4:32). Between us, I have a feeling that such sharing wasn't a very big deal for most of the early Christians. They were largely of the poorer classes, laboring people or folks with a family fishing business, and a fair number of them slaves. So when the writer of Acts tells us that Barnabas "sold a field that belonged to him, then brought the money and laid it at the apostles' feet" (Acts 4:37), I suspect it's also telling us that here was a gift quite out of the ordinary. I'm struck, too, by the way the giving is described: "laid . . . at the apostles' feet." The writer is conveying a quality of humility—a humility that was all the more impressive since the giver is presumably a property owner of some substance.

Although this opening picture of Barnabas is brief, we learn a good deal. He is a Levite—that is, a member of the tribe in Israel responsible for religious leadership; he's a native of Cyprus, which means that his family has been away from the homeland for a generation or more, and that although his name was Joseph, the apostles had given him the name Barnabas, meaning "son of encouragement" (Acts 4:36). If you're going to get a nickname, this is the kind to get! Most of us who have at some time been identified by something other than our birth name have usually gotten it by way of our appearance, a condensing of our given name, or a reminder of some special event in our lives—generally an embarrassing one. Apparently Barnabas was someone who was always encouraging people; wherever he went, people drew strength from him. What a great name! And let me say now, before we go farther in this man's story, that those who named him must have done so in a moment of high inspiration. It's as if they were predicting his holy career.

I have a feeling Barnabas exercised this ministry of encouragement on an everyday basis; if it hadn't been so, he wouldn't have been ready for the crucial instances. Such an instance arose sometime after Saul of Tarsus was converted. Saul had been a major persecutor of the young Christian movement. After his dramatic conversion he preached powerfully in Damascus, confounding those who didn't believe Jesus was the Messiah. In time, his opponents sought to kill him, so he went on to Jerusalem.

It was a logical move. The major leadership of the church was there; I suspect Paul cherished the opportunity to meet the leaders at first hand, and to tell them the miracle Christ had worked in his life. Unfortunately, they weren't as anxious to meet Saul as he was to meet them. As the writer puts it, "they were all afraid of him, for they did not believe that he was a disciple" (Acts 9:26).

I can't imagine a more devastating rebuke. These were Saul's new spiritual kin; he had admired them from a distance and no doubt longed to hear their stories of their firsthand knowledge of Jesus the Christ. Furthermore, Saul had already begun paying his dues, having just escaped martyrdom. And they were *afraid* of him! If Saul had been a converted alcoholic, this would have driven him back to the bottle. I see Saul in a lonely room in some public lodging, questioning almost everything: the saints in Jerusalem, the wisdom of the church's leaders, his place in the church, perhaps in the darkest moments even his conversion.

Enter the gardener. "But Barnabas took him, brought him to the apostles, and described for them how on the road he had seen the Lord, who had spoken to him, and how in Damascus he had spoken boldly in the name of Jesus" (Acts 9:27). When you write the history of the Christian faith, put these two words in italics: *But Barnabas.* This is a corner in the story which, if not turned, might have left the rest of the story foundering. Call it providence, call it the will of God, call it the work of the Holy Spirit, but never forget that a certain type of person was needed to effect this crucial moment—a gardener among human beings.

I don't think Barnabas told the disciples anything they hadn't already heard. It seems altogether likely that Saul had told some of his experiences for himself. But the disciples needed to hear it from someone whose witness was beyond dispute. Barnabas was that kind of person.

The next time the book of Acts mentions Barnabas, we get a summary reason for the persuasiveness that so marked him. Some unnamed believers from Cyrene and Cyprus carried the Christian message to the city of Antioch. There they made converts among not only the Jews, but also some Gentiles. This was at a time when the church was not yet sure that a non-Jew could be a Christian. Peter had reported such an instance in his ministry, but the leaders were still cautious—all the more so, I imagine, in the case at Antioch, since the persons leading the effort there were not people of Peter's stature. As I said a moment ago, they are unnamed. So the leaders in Jerusalem sent a reliable examiner to evaluate the situation—Barnabas. Now hear how Barnabas responded: "When he came and saw the grace of God, he rejoiced, and he exhorted them all to remain faithful to the Lord with steadfast devotion; *for he was a good man, full of the Holy Spirit and of faith*" (Acts 11:23–24). The italics are mine, but I can't help feeling that if italics had been available to the author of Acts, they would have appeared in the original manuscript.

Here's what impresses me so much. In the early church, everyone was expected to be "good . . . , full of the Holy Spirit and of faith." But obviously Barnabas brought special quality to these words. It is as if he were the walking definition. Theology needs walking definitions so badly, you know. The terms we deal with are all so qualitative and so difficult to define. Yes, there's a sense in which "beauty is in the eye of the beholder," but all of us also know there's more to it than that, and so too with goodness, kindness, humility, graciousness, joy, and peace. The dictionary definitions leave us unfulfilled, and so do the weighty, five-hundred-page philosophical discussions. But now and then we see a person who *is* the definition, and thereafter we don't struggle so hard for words. I believe Barnabas was like that; so when the writer of Acts wanted to tell his readers why the church leaders would choose this man to do this special job, he picked up words that everyone in the church knew and that all of them sought in their best days to fulfill, and said, "That's what Barnabas was like."

I'm glad they sent Barnabas to Antioch. "When he . . . saw the grace of God, he rejoiced." What wonderful good sense! Some see the grace of God and immediately establish a period of probation; others formulate a body of questions to be sure that what they have found meets some particular and peculiar standard; still others anticipate the problem it will be to orient these people into the larger body. Barnabas rejoiced. It isn't that he was superficial; he also "exhorted them all to remain faithful to the Lord with steadfast devotion" (Acts 11:23). I repeat, the apostolic leaders were in the Spirit when they sent Barnabas.

But there's more to it. When he saw the potential in Antioch, he "went to Tarsus to look for Saul" (Acts 11:25). I don't know what Saul was doing back in Tarsus, but something in me feels that it wasn't good. I don't mean that Saul was deserting the faith—he was far too stubborn for that. I just have the feeling that Saul was still finding his way. He had a calling, but he couldn't ascertain how to use it, and it seems likely that the church leaders weren't much help. Some of the most significant personalities in God's kingdom have been irregular individuals, hard for interviewing bodies to evaluate and even more difficult for administrators to direct. It's the very extent of the gifts in such persons that complicates using them; but it is also the extent of their gifts that—when the right place is found—makes these people geniuses. Saul of Tarsus was that kind of person, but I honestly don't think we'd know it yet today if it weren't for Barnabas. Barnabas "went to Tarsus to look for Saul."

They spent a year in Antioch "and taught a great many people, and it was in Antioch that the disciples were first called 'Christians' " (Acts 11:26). Then, when the leaders in Antioch were fasting and praying, "the Holy Spirit said, 'Set apart for me Barnabas and Saul for the work to which I have called them' " (Acts 13:2). They took with them a young associate who had joined them earlier, John Mark, son of a woman who was something of a leader in the church at Jerusalem—a woman of enough strength and influence that leaders of the church met in her home (Acts 12:12).

In the course of this missionary journey a number of notable things happened—miracles and confrontations with evil. And also some changes that are reported almost casually but that prove significant later. First, a change in Saul's name: "But Saul, also known as Paul," the writer says (Acts 13:9)—and from that time on we know him only as Paul. Then the team that was always known as "Barnabas and Saul" suddenly is referred to as "Paul and his companions" (Acts 13:13) or "Paul and Barnabas" (Acts 13:43 and thereafter). There's nothing very subtle about it; the mantle of leadership has passed. Then, in the report of the journey from Paphos to Perga, a laconic note: "John, however, left them and returned to Jerusalem" (Acts 13:13).

The continuing journey was a continuing triumph for Paul and Barnabas. Wherever they went, the Spirit of God was with them in power. They were so much a team that they didn't lose a step in the transition from "Barnabas and Saul" to "Paul and Barnabas." Meanwhile, an issue was brewing in the church: Could non-Jews be admitted into the church simply on their acceptance of Christ, or must they pass through rituals that would first identify them as Jews? The church met in council at Jerusalem to make one of the most significant decisions in all of its history. After reports from Simon Peter and from Barnabas and Paul (it's interesting that their names are listed in this order in the report from the council, where Barnabas no doubt had superior standing), the assembly voted for full acceptance of the Gentiles, and appointed "our beloved Barnabas and Paul" to deliver the word to the Gentile believers in Antioch, Syria, and Cilicia

Paul and Barnabas remained in Antioch for some time, again enjoying a fruitful ministry together. Then Paul suggested that they return to some of the cities where they had preached earlier. Barnabas agreed, adding that they should again take John Mark. Paul objected; John Mark "had deserted them in Pamphylia." Then a sad sentence: "The disagreement became so sharp that they parted company" (Acts 15:39). But the church apparently took in stride what troubles me so much. The writer reports that Barnabas took John Mark with him to Cyprus and that Paul chose Silas and set out, "the believers commending him to the grace of the Lord" as he went to Syria and Cilicia (Acts 15:39–41). Perhaps the early church believed enough in the character of both men to conclude that while they might disagree, they were nevertheless God's anointed servants. Or maybe they were realistic enough to recognize that even when we are most godly, we have to cope with our humanness. Or perhaps they simply believed that in spite of our strong opinions and our sometimes petty behavior, God continues to be at work.

I should tell you that I like Paul a very great deal. In fact, it's because I like him so much that he doesn't have a chapter in this book: if I ever write something about Paul, I want to write a whole book about him. But in this instance, my vote goes with Barnabas. I'm a great believer in second chances—perhaps because I've received so many. To be honest, I can't imagine Paul's arguing against John Mark without its occurring to him that God and Barnabas had been exceedingly patient with him, Paul, else he wouldn't be heading out on this journey with council approval. But Paul is a stubborn man; and I will acknowledge that this stubbornness of his is part of the secret of his achievements for the kingdom. But my vote here is with Barnabas.

This is the Barnabas who is a gardener among human beings. Because, as we saw in an earlier chapter, John Mark became—according to the best Christian tradition—the author of the Gospel according to Mark, the Gospel that is generally considered the first of the Gospels to be written and the Gospel that reflects the teaching of Simon Peter. And apparently Paul changed his mind years later. In Paul's Second Letter to Timothy, one of the last of the epistles attributed to Paul either directly or indirectly, Paul writes, "Get Mark and bring him with you, for he is useful in my ministry" (2 Tim. 4:11). I dare to venture we wouldn't have heard of Mark if Barnabas hadn't taken his fledgling plant, watered it, and turned it to the place where it would get just the right amount of sunshine—beginning in Cyprus as Barnabas's assistant.

And will you allow me one bit of pure speculation? When Paul pleaded with the people at Corinth to seek the best gift, love, and gave us what we now identify as "the love chapter," his First Letter to the Corinthians, chapter 13, I like to think that Barnabas was his model. When you write something as beautiful as that chapter, you need to have in mind some picture beyond simple imagining. An artist needs a pencil sketch before beginning a work in oil. I see Barnabas as Paul's pencil sketch. But I'm just imagining.

This, however, I suggest with some rather hard data. I wonder if we would have the epistles of Paul or the Gospel of Mark if there hadn't been a Barnabas. I wonder if both of these landmark figures would have been lost—in rejection, in Paul's case, or in fumbling immaturity, in the case of John Mark.

And I think again of the line from the days when Saul and Barnabas first preached in Antioch—that "it was in Antioch that the disciples were first called 'Christians' " (Acts 11:26). Some scholars feel, with good reason, that the people in Antioch used that term simply because Saul and Barnabas spoke so much about Jesus Christ that the people associated the name with them. Perhaps. But perhaps also, as listeners heard what Christ was like and what he taught, they said, "Just like these two men. Especially the less scholarly one."

Could be. At the very least, however, Barnabas was a very good gardener. The kind who made human plants flourish where otherwise they might die. Just ask Saul and John Mark—and hundreds of others, I venture, whose names we don't know.

Notes

CHAPTER 2: JUST AN ORDINARY MAN

1. Helen H. Lemmel, "Turn Your Eyes upon Jesus," *The United Methodist Hymnal* (Nashville: The United Methodist Publishing House, 1989), 349.

CHAPTER 4: THE MAN MOSES

1. Robert Alter, *The Five Books of Moses: A Translation with Commentary* (New York: W. W. Norton & Co., 2004), 300–301.

CHAPTER 6: MY FRIEND, ELIJAH

1. Frank Mason North, "Where Cross the Crowded Ways of Life," *The Methodist Hymnal* (Nashville: The Methodist Publishing House, 1966), 204.

2. *The Interpreter's Bible,* (New York and Nashville: Abingdon Press, 1954), 3:161.

CHAPTER 7: "STUBBORN OUNCES"

1. Howard Moss, "Amos," in *Congregation: Contemporary Writers Read the Jewish Bible,* ed. David Rosenberg (New York: Harcourt Brace Jovanovich, 1987), 210 .

2. Bonaro Overstreet, "Stubborn Ounces (To One Who Doubts the Worth of Doing Anything if You Can't Do Everything)," in *Hands Laid upon the Wind,* by Bonaro W. Overstreet (New York: W. W. Norton & Co., 1955), 15.

CHAPTER 8: FAITHFUL FOR THE LONG PULL

1. Phillip P. Bliss, "Dare to Be a Daniel," in *Ocean Grove Sings* (Franklin, TN: Providence House Publishers, 2000), #158.

CHAPTER 9: LIVING ON BORROWED TIME

1. T. S. Eliot, "A Song for Simeon," in T. S. Eliot, *The Complete Poems and Plays 1909–1950* (New York: Harcourt, Brace & Co., 1958), 69.

CHAPTER 14: YOUNG MAN IN A HURRY

1. William Barclay, *The Gospel of Mark* (Philadelphia: Westminster Press, 1956), xiii.
2. Tom Wright, *Mark for Everyone* (Louisville, KY: Westminster John Knox Press, 2004), 200.
3. Barclay, 365.
4. Barclay, xvii.
5. Eugene H. Peterson, *The Message:* The New Testament in Contemporary English (Colorado Springs, CO: NavPress, 1993), 74.

CHAPTER 16: "A GARDENER AMONG HUMAN BEINGS"

1. Katharine Butler Hathaway, *The Little Locksmith* (New York: Coward-McCann, 1943), 178–79.